JESUS
OUTSIDE THE GOSPELS

JESUS
OUTSIDE THE GOSPELS

R. Joseph Hoffmann

Prometheus Books
59 John Glenn Drive
Amherst, New York 14228-2197

Library of Congress Catalog Card No.: 84–42862

ISBN 13: 978-0-87975-387-0
ISBN 10: 0-87975-387-0

Printed in the United States of America on acid-free paper

CONTENTS

One

INTRODUCTION:
BETWEEN JESUS AND THE GOSPELS

The Gospel account of Jesus in the New Testament is not an objective representation of events but a tale fashioned *after* a specific doctrine *about* Jesus had begun to supersede and displace historical details. That this is so is hardly surprising: the domestic habits of a man who was believed to have risen from the grave could hardly be as memorable as his alleged healing powers, his predictions (if there were such) of his death and resurrection, or the circumstances of his supposedly miraculous birth. The Gospels, written some two generations (more or less) after the events they describe are not—and were not intended to be—biographies. In their own time, they developed as the missionary propaganda of the cult of Christ, and were written down by believers whose concern was twofold: (1) to document their conviction that the risen Lord had been the Messiah (Greek, *Christos*), especially through a highly selective use of Old Testament prophecy, and (2) to persuade others to join them in their belief. Paul, a convert to the Christian cause in the 30s, shortly after the crucifixion, writes some twenty-five years after the death of Jesus:

> Christ died for our sins in accordance with scripture [that is, the Old Testament], he was buried, and raised the third day in accordance with the scripture. . . . If Christ had not been raised, then our preaching is in vain and your faith is in vain. [1 Cor. 15:3, 4, 14]

Here the nuclei of the central doctrines of later Christianity are already present: The death of Jesus is a redemptive sacrifice, a price paid to a pawnbroker of a devil for the release of human souls; it was carried out as part of a divine plan that could be learned by reading the Hebrew scriptures, especially the prophets and the psalms. Most

7

important, his death had not been final, merely a temporary concession to the powers of darkness (archons) who rule the world. Everything hinges for Paul and his converts on the *resurrection,* the core of his gospel and the warrant for his faith.

Paul was in the habit of preaching doctrine (though in a highly unsystematic way) well before the time the Gospels took shape. The best guess is that the earliest of his letters (1 Thessalonians, c. 50) predates the earliest written Gospel by a generation. Put the other way around, no Gospel took shape until after certain dogmatic propositions had become a part of the preaching of early Christian missionaries. And while the Gospels reflect these propositions in different ways and with various emphases, *no* Gospel exists that has not been colored—indeed suffused—by the beliefs of the Jesus cult. It need hardly be pointed out that the interests of missionaries do not usually include impartial or factual reporting.

Two

THE DELAY IN WRITING THE GOSPELS

Why were no Gospels written in Jesus' lifetime, and what are the reasons for a delay of fifty years or more between his death and the received gospel that invests it with meaning and saves it from becoming a "stumbling block" and "foolishness" (1 Cor. 1:23)? To answer this, we must examine in some detail the intentions of Jesus and those of his followers. As we shall see, these intentions do not always coincide.

The Intention of Jesus

Jesus did not found a church, nor did he intend to start a scribal community charged with the responsibility of preserving and transmitting his teaching. Recent studies have made it clear that the Jesus cult was an offshoot of the movement associated with John the Baptist, differing from it in terms of ritual law and practice, but closely resembling it in belief and outlook. The Gospels are surprisingly rich in references that permit us to chart the debts of the Jesus-movement to John and his disciples, as well as to the hostility that emerged between the two groups over the question of baptism (cf. Matt. 11:2-19). According to Matthew 10:7, the newly appointed disciples are told to preach, "The kingdom of heaven is at hand," a message that does not differ in kind from the one attributed to John in Matthew 3:2, nor from the one assigned to Jesus after John's arrest (Matt. 4:17).

The message itself—the coming of the *basileia tou Theou* (the exercise of the power of God)—is firmly rooted in Jewish apocalyptic thought, and has little to do with the Renaissance ideas of kingship and kingdom imposed on the text by King James' translators in 1611. The core of Jesus' message is one he inherited from his own teacher and shared with his followers, many of whom embraced the Jesus cult after John's arrest. Furthermore, the message about the kingdom of God did not originate with John the Baptist, and though forced into the background of Christian teaching by an unforeseen transplantation of the gospel into non-Jewish soil, it does not end with Jesus.

The roots of the concept "Kingdom of God" are political (Psalms 97, 99). In the Jewish thought of the time, God was thought of as a ruler whose reign on earth was thwarted by the existence of heathen empires. This concept survives today, especially among Moslems, in the distinction between the *Dar-al-harab* (territory not yet surrendered to God) and the *Dar-al-Islam* (territory surrendered to God). In the Judaism of the first century, it was widely supposed that the kingship of God over the heathen territories would finally be brought to fulfillment in a day of judgment (or "Day of the Lord"). Those who were righteous would reap material blessings on the appointed day (Enoch 10:17 ff.); the wicked, especially those who had opposed the expansion of the kingdom or disbelieved in the power of the God of Israel, would be overthrown.

Fortunately, we possess a large volume of Jewish speculation about the coming of the "Day of the Lord" and the signs that were supposed to precede it: in the Bible, the Book of Daniel and certain sections of Zechariah, Isaiah, and Ezekiel; outside the canonical scriptures the Testaments of the Twelve Patriarchs, Enoch, 4 Ezra (especially 4:22-43), and the Damascus Document. The last of these, dating from the first century CE, begins with a verse that may be considered thematic: "Listen all you who know righteousness and understand the works of God. For he has a controversy with all flesh and will execute judgment upon all who despise him." The Dead Sea or Qumran Community produced a number of documents that illustrate the apocalyptic beliefs of sectarian Jews in the first century. Many of these now exist in good translations,[1] and raise questions—even if they do not yield answers—about the relation of John the Baptist and Jesus to the apocalyptic sect known as Essenes (pious ones).

Graphic speculation about the coming of the Day of the Lord remained primarily a sectarian phenomenon in Judaism. In 4 Ezra, transcribed in the first century CE and preserved in Christian circles, such speculation dominates:

> Behold, the days come when the inhabitants of the earth shall be seized with great panic. . . . then shall the sun suddenly shine forth by night and the moon by day, and blood shall trickle forth from wood and the stone utter its voice. . . . The wild beasts shall desert their haunts, and women bear monsters. The one-year-old children shall speak with their voices; pregnant women shall bring forth untimely births at three or four months and these shall live and dance. [5:1-8]

Comparable imagery can be found in the Book of Daniel (Chapters 7-12), and in apocryphal literature. The more striking parallels, however, are not in the Old Testament or the Apocrypha, but in the New Testament:

> When you hear of wars and rumours of wars, do not be alarmed. This must take place, but the end is not yet. For nation will rise against nation, and kingdom against kingdom. There will be earthquakes in various places, there will be famines. [Mark 13:7-8]

And in Matthew:

> When you see the desolating sacrilege spoken of by the prophet Daniel, standing in the holy place . . . then let those who are in Judaea flee to the mountains. . . . alas for those who are with child and for those who give suck in those days . . . . Immediately after the tribulation of those days the sun will be darkened and the moon will not give its light and the stars will fall from heaven and the powers of the heavens will be shaken; then will appear the sign of the Son of Man in heaven and then all the tribes of the earth will mourn and they will see the Son of Man coming on the clouds of heaven with power and great glory; and he will send out his angels with a loud trumpet call, and they will gather his elect from the four winds, from one end of heaven to the other. [Matt. 24:15, 16, 19, 29-31]

Regardless of whether these words belong to Jesus, they express a central belief of his early followers and almost certainly contain an element of his message. As far as we can determine, this was not a message *about* himself, but a message about the coming day of judgment on which the Son of Man *(huios tou anthropou)*, an obscure apocalyptic figure described in Daniel 7:13-15, would be licensed by God to take over direct control of a new kingdom (cf. Mark 14:62). *The failure of these signs to materialize led to the curious result that Jesus was retroactively declared "Son of Man"* (as well as Christ, Messiah) by his followers after his death, and the "signs," together with his reappearance *(parousia)*, were projected into the future. In this way, the unfulfilled message of the Last Days was preserved on the reckoning that Jesus, in speaking of the Son of Man, was misunderstood, that he had been speaking of *himself* and further that he had to die and be glorified *prior* to his return (Luke 22:69). The anguishing hiatus between belief and fact, expectation and fulfillment, was explained away by contriving a parallel gap between Jesus' pronouncements and the understanding of his associates:

1. "He began to teach them that the Son of Man must suffer many things . . . and be killed and after three days rise again" (Mark 8:31; Luke 9:22, changed to direct discourse).

2. "'The Son of man is to be delivered into the hands of men' . . . But they did not understand this saying" (Mark 9:31-32).

3. "The Son of Man will be delivered to the chief priests and the scribes, and they will condemn him to death and deliver him to the gentiles; and they will mock him and spit upon him and scourge him and kill him; and after three days he will rise" (Mark 10:33-34).

By this "triple attestation"—a primitive way of giving irrefragable proof of an occurrence—the early church was able to explain two things to itself and to would-be converts. First—and most important—that Jesus' passion had not been an accident, but rather part of a divine plan for redemption. Jesus had foretold his death on several occasions and was misunderstood in each case. His death was unforeseen only by his disciples, who later "remembered" that Jesus had predicted (Luke 24:45-49) how he would die. Second, the early church predicated this suffering, not of someone who merely *foretold* the coming of the Son of Man but of someone who foretold—in each case—that the Son of Man *would suffer and die.* By this logic, there could be little doubt that Jesus was speaking of none other than himself: he alone fit the description put forward by his believers.

As far as the Jews were concerned, the logic was unpersuasive. Accustomed to arguing from scripture, they challenged the Christian missionaries to show where it was predicted that the Messiah should die the death of an outcast. The Christian response was a masterful concoction of Old Testament texts[2]—all of it the stuff of Christian doctrine and oratorio, but in its time irrelevant to Jewish messianic expectations. For his followers, Jesus had been the Son of Man; following a period of glorification, seated at his father's right hand, he would come again to sit in judgment on the enemies of God (Acts 2:17-39). For the opponents of the Jesus cult, the preaching of a crucified god was merely ludicrous (1 Cor. 1:23).

The Beliefs of Jesus vs. Beliefs About Jesus

It is not easy to separate the beliefs of Jesus about the kingdom from his followers' attempts to portray him as the apocalyptic judge and Messiah. German critics from the beginning of the century used two slogans to express the problem that New Testament critics face in their search for the Jesus of history: "The proclaimer became the proclaimed"; and "Jesus announced the kingdom, and the church came instead." Despite the difficulties implicit in these expressions, we can say with some certainty that Jesus, like John before him, shared the apocalyptic hopes of the Jews of his time. *He did not regard himself as the Son of Man, but as a continuator of the Baptist's message of repentance.* Further, he almost certainly believed and announced that the Day of the Lord would be preceded by certain signs (see Mark 13:24-31), and that the birth pangs of the Last Days would occur in his own lifetime.

In documenting these conclusions, we must approach the Gospels in an almost archaeological way as strata or layers of traditions. In the course of time, the message of Jesus was altered to conform to what was believed *about* him (The proclaimer became the proclaimed). What experience had disconfirmed was suppressed, erased (not always possible with firmly rooted tradition),[3] and frequently revised.

1. Such is the case with Jesus' own words about the Kingdom of God and his own Second Coming. If we take the Kingdom of God as the central portion of the message proclaimed by Jesus, then we will want to know when Jesus *himself* thought the Son of Man would come and the judgment occur. In an unerased and probably unerasable section of Mark's Gospel (13:30-32), Jesus is given to say, "Truly I say to you this generation will not pass away before all these things [that is, signs] take place." That this verse is very ancient—perhaps an authentic saying of Jesus—can be defended on what New Testament scholars call the "dissimilarity principle." By this is meant a verse whose existence and survival cannot be explained in terms of the experience of the early church, or better, something remembered in spite of there being every reason to forget or suppress the memory. The signs of the last days did *not* take place, as Jesus had foretold, within the lifetime of his followers, but the fact that he made such a prediction was "traditioned" from a very early period.

A similar saying is preserved in Matthew 10:23, where the troubles confronting the early church are read back into the teaching of Jesus: "I say to you, you will not have gone through all the towns of Israel before the Son of Man comes." The early memories of the persecuted Jesus sect included the data that their vindication—the return of Jesus as the Son of Man and judge of all who had rejected them (Mark 13:13)—was something they would all live to see. They remembered that such a promise had been made to Jesus' closest followers, and they staked their faith on this collective expectation. At least part of the early zeal of the Christian missionary movement can be explained by the primitive belief that time was hastening to a close and that Jesus would reappear imminently to fulfill his promise (see Rev. 22:20; 1 Cor. 16:22).

2. It is the attachment of the missionary endeavor to the *schedule* of the Second Coming that explains the next stratum in the tradition: Jesus himself had clearly predicted the coming of the Kingdom within

the lifetime of his hearers, indeed probably his own. John the Baptist had preached the same thing (Matt. 3:10-12), and many of his followers, true to his message, attached themselves to John's successor (John 1:37; cf. 5:31 ff.) after the Baptist's execution for political dissidence.[4] Many of his followers must have regarded Jesus as the "true" Messiah following the death of their master and what was perhaps a certain feeling that their apocalyptic hopes had been betrayed. John thus becomes, in the Gospel tradition, a prophetic forerunner, the proclaimer of Jesus, who then displaced the Baptist as the focus of apocalyptic expectation. The early church assigned John the role of eschatological prophet—the one sent to prepare the way of the Lord.[5] Yet John's real influence was initially independent of the Jesus movement, and probably included a sect that survived for some time after his death and was hostile to the Christians.[6] His importance is highlighted in Mark 6:14-16, where a frightened Herod can think of no better explanation for Jesus' powers than that he is John redivivus, a verse that indicates that the early Christians were in the habit of comparing the two prophets in their missionary propaganda.

3. The death of Jesus in circumstances not very different from John's[7]—indeed much closer than the Gospels suggest—would have been seen as a shattering disproof of the imminent coming of the Day of the Lord. *The crucifixion stood as a flat contradiction of Jesus' own expectations and those of his disciples.* To miss this point is to miss the driving force behind the later development of Christian propaganda. As the community theorized that Jesus had been speaking of himself as the Son of Man, destined by God to suffer, die, and be raised, they effectively managed to postpone the Day of the Lord. This postponement, in fact, was coordinated with the missionary work of the Jesus-believers and was soon understood as a concession granted by God to the missionaries; that is, the Day of the Lord would not come *until* such time as the gospel had been preached (2 Peter 3:9).

In the Gospels, this postponement is reflected in an ever-widening geographical circle: Jesus himself envisioned a preaching mission to a few Galilean towns; his disciples at first expected that the end would come before the Kingdom was proclaimed throughout Israel (Matt. 10:23). When this too failed, the explanation quite naturally became that Jesus, now enthroned as the Son of Man, must have intended the gospel to be preached *beyond* the limits of the Jewish world—even to Gentiles. Thus, they read back into his teaching (as it happens, his "post-resurrection" teaching) a mandate to evangelize the nations (Matt. 28:19). That the Day of the Lord had still not come, despite the success of the missionaries, was always explained by the rationale that the preaching of the gospel—increasingly confused with teaching *about* the founder—had not been carried out to the founder's specifications. Put simply, the delay of the Day of the Lord was ascribed to the ever-expanding need to announce its coming, a rationalization that still holds sway among some Christian sects.[8]

The Epistles of Paul and the Hopes of the Cult

The genuine letters of Paul[9] offer us the earliest, but by no means an immaculate, record of the hopes of the early Jesus-believers. If there is any truth to the textbook chronology of his life, Paul became a convert to Christianity not long after the death of Jesus—perhaps in the 30s—having worked for a while as an agent of the synagogue to check the growth of the Jesus-movement. From the first, he seems to have preached a "gospel" more suitable for Gentile listeners than for Jewish converts—not surprising since his conversion would surely have resulted in alienation from his Jewish associates. At any rate, the gospel he preached was not readily—at least not immediately—endorsed by the Jewish-Christian circles in Jerusalem with whom Paul quarreled almost from the start of his ministry. The Corinthian letters and the letter to the Galatians reflect a bitter contest between Paul and the Jerusalem apostles over the very substance of the Christian message; wherever Paul preached, he was up against one or more "gospels," each purported to be the "gospel of Christ." Paul, doubtless like all the rest, claimed to have the only true gospel, and carps at the salvation-hungry Christian communities for allowing "false apostles" to preach to them (see 2 Cor. 11:12 ff.).

It is hardly surprising that this controversy between Paul and Jerusalem arose. Jewish Christianity remained a fundamentally apocalyptic movement for some time after Jesus' death; its earliest message was a message about the coming of a catastrophe, the final battle between good and evil and the judgment of the world by a glorified Jesus (Acts 2:14-21). This message was not written but oral; it constituted the "Word of the Lord" delivered to the disciples and preached, initially, to a Jewish world that prized the living oral tradition above anything written. It is instructive in this regard to remember that the "canon" of Old Testament writings was not settled until around AD 100 at Jamnia (Jabneh), and the New Testament canon not before the fourth century. The average person in the first century did not share our modern infatuation with the authority of the printed word; most, if not all of what he knew, he knew by tradition and word of mouth.

Paul, as a Pharisee, shared the apocalyptic hopes of the newly formed community of the last days. He participated in their communal meals *(eucharistia)* and was fully persuaded that the Day of the Lord was at hand. But we can trace a shift in Paul's thinking: a transition from rather primitive ideas about the timing of the return of Jesus (1 Thess.) to a fully Hellenized view of Jesus, in which his Resurrection and not his return became the central datum of Christian belief (1 and 2 Cor.). While Paul never loses sight of the *parousia*—the reappearance of Jesus—it pales by comparison with his belief that *the crucifixion was God's way of overcoming the powers of sin and death*—a victory certified in the Resurrection. Put simply, Paul transposed the eschatological battle between God and Satan back into the life of Jesus, making a future cosmic battle—thus the signs of the *eschaton*—unnecessary. In a mythological scenario still embedded in the so-called "Apostle's Creed" and given scriptural expression in 1 Peter 3:19,[10] Jesus, between the time of the crucifixion and the resurrection, had descended into Hell and harrowed its precincts, bound Satan, and established himself as king of heaven and earth. This idea of an apocalyptic battle is prominent in many ancient Near Eastern myths, notably in the stories of Osiris and Tammuz. Both the scribes of Qumran and the author of the Epistle to the Ephesians preserve the old Zoroastrian belief in a cosmic battle between the powers of good and evil to decide the fate of mankind.

Paul seems also to have shared the doubts of his converts about the actual time of Jesus' return. This and the fact that the local Christian congregations freely entertained such doubts (see 2 Peter 3:4-13) help us to understand why it became necessary to emphasize more and more the purely theoretical notion that the "signs" of the Last Day and the birthpangs of the new age belonged to the past rather than to the future. Such is the situation we find reflected in what is probably the earliest piece of Christian literature, Paul's letter to the Jesus cult in Thessalonica.

There Paul responds to questions addressed to him by an increasingly skeptical congregation. Some members of the community have died—before the Day of the Lord, and seemingly in spite of Paul's guarantees to his converts. How can this delay be squared with the message that Paul preached to them at the time of their conversion—that they would live to see the return of the Son of Man? Paul's answer makes the crucial shift from *eschatological* thinking—that is, concentration on the signs and time of the eschaton—to *christological* thinking: what Jesus has already accomplished and who he *must* be to accomplish it. Put bluntly, the waning of eschatology, brought on by a pattern of delay followed by further rationalization, is the single most important fact in the elevation of the historical Jesus to the status of a divine being.

In addressing the Thessalonians, Paul writes:

> About dates and times [of the end] we need not write to you, for you know perfectly well that the day of the Lord comes like a thief in the night. While they are talking of peace and security all at once calamity comes in upon them, sudden as the pangs that come upon a woman with child. [1 Thess. 5:1-3]

Paul's own view at this point in his career was still relatively mythological: he believed, for example, that there would be a summons from an archangel, followed by a trumpet call (the practice in Rome prior to the entrance of the emperor), a descent of the Lord from heaven, and a resurrection of the dead in which the Christian dead, as a reward for their perseverance, would rise first (1 Thess. 4:15-16).

Evidently, the assurance that those who had died without seeing the calamity would be the first awakened on the Day of the Lord was unpersuasive to the Thessalonians. Some years later, after Paul's death, a second letter addressed to the Thessalonians in Paul's name offers a rather different set of assurances and explanations for the delay:

> Now brothers, about the coming of Our Lord Jesus Christ and his gathering of us to himself, I beg you do not suddenly lose your heads and alarm yourselves . . . [for] that day cannot come before the final rebellion against God, when wickedness will be revealed in human form, the man doomed to perdition. He is the enemy. He rises in his pride against every god so called, every object of men's worship and even takes his seat in the temple of God. [2 Thess. 2:1-4]

This passage was probably written soon after the destruction of Jerusalem by the Roman forces under Titus in 68-70. The "man doomed to perdition" who considers himself a god is doubtless Vespasian, Nero's successor, who had presided over the early skirmishes with the Jews in Galilee.

Vespasian was proclaimed emperor in 69, and in the manner of Hellenistic rulers from Alexander onward, he expected tribute to be paid to his image and to the recognized gods of Rome. Indeed, the failure of the Jews to honor the emperor's image was a long-standing source of contention between Rome and Judea; Pontius Pilate had failed to introduce the emperor cult in 30, yielding before the thrust of rebellion. Vespasian effected by force what Pilate could not achieve by trickery.[11]

Obviously, the author of 2 Thessalonians believes the Day of the Lord is still to come. But by the time he writes, fully forty years or more have elapsed since the death of Jesus, and at least two decades since Paul had first written to the Thessalonian community to voice his own confidence with the words, "We who are alive, who are left until the coming of the Lord, shall not forestall those who have died (1 Thess. 4:15). There is no such suggestion in 2 Thessalonians; rather, a complaint about apocalyptic enthusiasts who think the Day has arrived or is about to dawn (2 Thess. 2:2-3) and a declaration that something—known to the author as the "Restrainer," but probably to be identified with the incarnate power of evil, the emperor—will disappear from the scene (2 Thess. 2:8). In short, the author has said that the Lord will not come while the empire endures, thus making the end of time dependent on the political fortunes of the empire itself. When the day does come, it will mean persecution for the Romans (that is, an inversion of the political situation) and a reward for the persecuted Christians (1 Thess. 1:5-10). This idea is more elaborately expressed in the book of Revelation (16:5-7).

The Signs of the Last Days

So far we have seen that the continuing delay of the *parousia* was explained in three ways. (1) At the most primitive level, there was speculation that the glorification of Jesus took time, and that once his otherwordly enthronement was accomplished, he would return as Son of Man to finish the work he had begun during his lifetime. This rationale must have been fairly short-lived and gave way to other explanations, namely, (2) Jesus must have intended for his message to be preached to Jews *and* Gentiles (see Acts 1:6-8). Only when this had been done would the end come. This solution provided a relatively open-ended excuse for the delay, though it stood in blatant contradiction to what Jesus himself had preached. (3) The end could not come until the earthly power of evil (Rome), the restraining force, had been overcome by the power of good (Christianity). Essentially, this was a deduction from (2), but made the timing of the *eschaton* contingent on the result of the Christian mission rather than on preaching alone.

There is a final element to the list of solutions offered by early Christians to the problem of the delay. This has to do with the *signs* expected to precede the Last Days. As we saw, Jewish apocalyptic literature and the New Testament literature standing in its train is rich in such signs. But because much apocalyptic literature—the Book of Revelation included—frequently uses these "signs" to refer to contemporary political events[12] rather than as literal images of future happenings, it is difficult to determine the attitude of Jesus and his followers to these harbingers of doom.

Conjoined in the Gospels are words that indicate Jesus shared the belief of his contemporaries that the Day of the Lord would be preceded by certain cataclysms, and a church-tradition, based on unfulfilled expectations, that openly disparages looking for signs. For example, in Mark 13:21, Jesus is given to prophesy days of distress and the coming of false messiahs and imposters, all of which are images flexible enough to suit almost any situation the fledgling church might confront. The reference point of such images is the present and the recent past (c. 70 AD), reflecting as they do the historical circumstances of the early missionaries in their contest with other sects and the synagogues. So, too, the reference to the "abomination of desolation" in Mark 13:14 (echoing Daniel 9:27) almost certainly presupposes the plundering of the Temple by the Roman forces under Titus in August of 70, thus indicating that the author of Mark's Gospel interpreted the burning of the Temple as a sure sign that the end was in progress. Yet this event, as we have seen, is nearly two generations removed from the lifetime of Jesus.

Alongside these obviously political "signs," added to the Gospels to give the impression of historical verisimilitude, are a number of purely imaginative ones that have no clear political or historical import: images of gloom and cosmic warfare thought to precede the coming of the Son of Man (Mark 13:24-27; cf. Matt. 24:28-31). Both sorts of images—political and literary—derive from Old Testament apocalyptic and apocryphal sources. But it is clear that the *political* forecasts, put in Jesus' mouth as prophecies of the end-time (see Luke 21:20), do not actually date from his lifetime. They reflect rather the conviction of the Jesus-believers that the fall of Jerusalem was a likely harbinger of a cataclysm soon to come. The grotesque portents—the signs in the heavens—would soon follow: "The present heaven and earth," writes the author of 2 Peter, "have been kept in store for burning . . . on the Day of the Lord, the heavens will disappear with a great rushing sound, the elements will disintegrate in flames, and the earth with all that is in it will be laid bare" (3:7, 10).

It is impossible to say whether Jesus used vivid apocalyptic descriptions in talking about the end-time, and there was no agreement in the early church about whether he had instructed his disciples in the art of eschatological forecasting. Whether he did or not, the Jesus-believers soon began openly to disparage looking for signs and preferred the idea that the Day would come when people least expected it (2 Peter 3:10). Paul offers this to the Thessalonians as a truism (1 Thess. 5:2), and the Gospels inconsistently ascribe the disparagement of signs to Jesus himself. Thus, immediately following the rather specific catalogue of portents in Mark 13:21-29 and the glum assurance that "the present generation will live to see it all" (Mark 13:30), we find the hand of the church at work, qualifying and softening the prediction: "About that day or that hour no one knows, not even the angels in heaven, not even the Son; only the Father" (Mark 13:32).

Hence a further way to explain the delay (though it flies in the face of later trinitarian beliefs about the omniscience of the Son and is omitted by Matthew and Luke) was to say that even Jesus had not known when the day was coming. To "expect" it (Mark 13:33-35) meant something less than to look for it, since—almost inevitably at the end of this line of development—the kingdom of God was "not coming with signs to be observed," and no sign would be given to this generation (Mark 8:11-12). In unresolved tension, the Gospels present Jesus announcing specific times and signs (Luke 12:49-56; 17:22-37; 21:25-31), rejecting all such speculation (Mark 8:12), and, in an obviously later stratum and a revision of Mark, proclaiming that "only the sign of Jonah" would precede the Last Days (Luke 11:29-32; Matt. 12:38-42). Matthew and Luke, however, present contradictory interpretations of what the sign of Jonah might be: for Luke, it refers to Jonah's judgment of the Ninevites; while for Matthew, Jonah's time in the whale's belly foreshadows the Resurrection. Hence, Matthew thinks of the Resurrection as a sign that the Last Days have arrived. For Luke, proleptically, the coming of the kingdom cannot be "observed" because "in fact it is already among you" (Luke 17:21).

The Problem of Disconfirmation

It has been necessary to stress the fact that early Christianity was an apocalyptic movement: Jesus, a follower of John the Baptist, preached a gospel—a message—of repentance in the conviction that he and his followers were living in the Last Days. John had become a victim of this teaching, charged with preaching a puritanical enthusiasm that almost certainly involved hostility toward the imperial authorities and Herod Antipas. Jesus, while enlarging the scope of John's mission (Luke 7:33-35) to include the outcasts of Jewish society, followed the same path to execution, charged with "stirring up the people" (Luke 23:5).

This unforeseen event determined the shape of the Jesus-believers' memory of their master: he became, in retrospect, the apocalyptic judge and Christ whose coming he himself had foretold. The coming Day of the Lord would be the day of his reappearance; the judgment doled out on that day would be his judgment on disbelievers. "There will be great distress in the land and a terrible judgment on the people" (Luke 21:23; cf. Matt. 23:1-36). "The Son of Man is to come in the glory of his Father and then he will repay every man what he has done. I say to you truly, there are some standing here who will not taste death before they see the Son of Man coming and his kingdom" (Matt. 16:27-28).

The first "Christians" also believed that the persecutions they suffered for holding to the message that Jesus had been the promised Son of Man was the first sign that the Day of the Lord was dawning. Punished and then expelled from the synagogues for their heresy, they charged the Jews with a pattern of hostility to the truth and identified their position under fire with that of the Old Testament prophets (Matt. 10:17-25; 23:34-36; Mark 13:9-13; cf. Luke 21:12-17).

O Jerusalem, Jerusalem, killing the prophets and stoning those who are sent to you. . . . Behold your Temple is forsaken and desolate. For I tell you, you will not see me again until you say "Blessed is he who comes in the name of the Lord." [Matt. 23:37, 38, 39]

Woe to you, Scribes and Pharisees, hypocrites! For you build the tombs of the prophets. . . . You witness against yourselves that you are the sons of those who murdered the prophets. [Matt. 23:29, 31; cf. Gen. 4:8; 2 Chron. 24:20-1; Zech. 1:1]

With such words, the Jesus-believers pronounced their own judgment on the history of Israel and located the crucifixion of Jesus within their cultic view of this history. Almost from the first, they were in the habit of searching scripture for explanations of Jesus' untimely death and for their own parlous status vis-à-vis the synagogue, such that their very *perception* of Jesus was to some extent shaped by their eccentric biblical exegesis—their conviction that he had been spoken of by the prophets whose fate he shared.[13]

We need not linger over the unhappy details of the relationship between the synagogue and the Jesus cult. Doubtless there were excesses on both sides, if there is a kernel of truth (and only that) to the story of the stoning of Stephen—after what is admittedly a long-winded and outrageous confession: "You stiffnecked people. . . . As your fathers did, so do you. Which of the prophets did not your fathers persecute? And they announced beforehand the coming of the Righteous One, whom you have now betrayed and murdered" (Acts 7:51-52). It is certainly true that first-century Jerusalem Christians lived in constant fear of reprisal from the Jews for their religious convictions.

It is hardly less likely that these early Christians disagreed among themselves concerning what to believe about Jesus and how much to profess in the open: Stephen's mistake appears to have been a lack of discretion (Acts 7:1-14) rather than his adherence to the Jesus cult. On the other side, the Christians never tired of reconstructing the history of Israel to suit their strange messianic beliefs (Acts 7) and of accusing the Jews of killing the Messiah (Acts 2:23; 2:36; 3:14; 4:10-11; 7:52). The regrettable climax of this war between synagogue and cult comes in a passage in 1 Thessalonians—assuredly not by Paul but inserted by a later editor of his letter: "The Jews killed both the Lord Jesus and the prophets . . . and displease God and oppose all men" (1 Thess. 2:15).

Jewish hostility toward the Jesus cult was actually a residual effect of the Christian proclamation itself. It is seldom observed that from the standpoint of Jewish theologians in the first century, Jesus' curriculum vitae was remarkably deficient in a Messiah's credentials. Misled by the ingenuity of the Gospel-writers' prooftexting, contemporary Christians are not always aware of the founder's inadequacy from the Jewish standpoint: Jesus was a Nazarene; the Messiah was expected to be Judean. He was not from David's line, a deficiency the Gospels labor to remove, then contradict with a doctrine of virgin birth. The Messiah would restore the kingdom of Israel, a mission the early believers insisted Jesus had rejected (Acts 1:6; John 18:36). Most damaging of all—despite the elaborate use of Old Testament passages to support their position—no Jew of Jesus' day would have expected the Messiah to die. Fewer still—even those like the Pharisees, who believed in bodily resurrection—would have seen the Resurrection as support for a messianic claim.

In short, the use of Old Testament passages in the Gospels was undertaken for propagandistic purposes; its use is tactical, a means of persuading potential Jewish converts that Jesus had in fact been the expected Messiah. In the main, however, this use of scripture would have seemed as eccentric and blasphemous to a Jewish fundamentalist of Jesus' day as the Reverend Sun Myung Moon's exegesis of the Bible seems to the Vatican. In an awkward attempt to explain why the Jews should have rejected their own Messiah, the Pauline author of Romans 9-11 puts forward the absurd theory that their action was God's means of bringing salvation to the Gentiles—an accomplishment which in due course would "stir Israel to emulation."

As we have seen, a further impediment to the Christian position was the problem of disconfirmation: "The time will come when you will long to see one of the days of the Son of Man" (Luke 17:22-23). Jesus' imaginary dialogues with the Pharisees, who demand he tell them when the kingdom is coming (Luke 17:20) is certainly "historical," but not in the sense of belonging to the biography of Jesus. Instead, Luke gives us a glimpse of the confrontation between cult and synagogue. For the synagogue, the failure of Jesus' promise must have seemed a persuasive case against any notion that he had been the Messiah, or had secretly inaugurated the kingdom during his lifetime (Luke 17:20). In the reply Luke places on Jesus' lips ("The Kingdom of God is not coming with signs to be observed,") we have a late first- or perhaps early second-century reply to a demand that is not hard hypothetically to reconstruct: "What persuades you Christians that the Kingdom is on its way, since all the signs are lacking?" (see 2 Peter 3:4). Despite the psychological effectiveness of the belief that the kingdom

would come unexpectedly—itself a flat contradiction of the apocalyptic prophecies scattered through the Gospels—we can nonetheless
detect a sense of eschatological urgency in Luke's rendition of the
Lord's Prayer:

> Father,
> Your name is holy:
> Let your Kingdom come,
> And give us bread for today.
>
> [Luke 11:2-3]

The kingdom did not come, at least not in the way and at the time
Jesus anticipated. *It is precisely this lacuna between early hope and
prolonged disappointment that provided the soil for belief in a spiritual Jesus*—legends about his birth, ministry, message, and conquest
of death—to take root. Anecdotes about Jesus, sayings attributed to
him, and miracles refashioned from Hellenistic literature to show his
spectacular powers took shape against the background of disappointment, persecution, rhetorical, and sometimes physical conflict.

From Tradition to Gospel

The question at hand however is the bearing of this background on the
writing of the Gospels. To repeat the question raised at the beginning
of this survey: Why were no contemporary records made of a man
whose teaching, message, and influence have endured for so long?
Obviously, in asking that sort of question we are permitting contemporary assumptions to get in the way of historical inquiry, or perhaps
more accurately, putting the verdict before the trial. In order to understand why the first century yields no verbatim transcript of Jesus'
sayings, no eyewitness account of his deeds or objective report of his
day-to-day activities, we must know something about the first century,
and something about the "traditioning" process—the causes determining how, why, and in what condition the stories about Jesus passed

from oral to written form.[14] Here I will mention only the more significant impediments to the writing of the Gospels in the years immediately following Jesus' death.

WORLD-VIEW

We began with the fact that Jesus preached the imminent end of the world, and that this belief was shared by his disciples. As a matter of course, people who accepted Jesus' message, or the literate among them, would not have written the story of his life and teachings since no generation would survive to read it. People confronted with the Day of the Lord would not have entertained the idea of writing history, and in fact, the Gospels, though late, give no indication that a written gospel *(evangelion)* was ever part of Jesus' intention. Paul's references to the "gospel" are always to what is *preached,* never to a written source.

THE MEDIUM OF THE GOSPEL

The early believers, having concluded that Jesus would soon return in the role of the Son of Man to pronounce judgment, were driven by a sense of urgency: the Son would reappear before the message had spread throughout Israel (Matt. 10:23). At this level of development, a definite geographical and temporal limit was envisioned. The mission, however, is a preaching enterprise, not a literary one. The belief that the end was coming soon meant that word of mouth was the only suitable way to spread the news of the kingdom. The Gospel of Mark recollects that "They went out and preached that men should repent" (Mark 6:12), following Jesus' example: "[He] went about all the cities and villages teaching in the synagogues and preaching the gospel of the Kingdom" (Matt. 9:35). Elsewhere, Jesus is remembered as charging his disciples: "Preach as you go, saying the Kingdom of heaven is at hand" (Matt. 10:7).

The primitive tradition that his followers were to preach only to the Jews suggests again the geographical limits of the mission. Accordingly, the early missionaries did not write gospels or biographies, precisely because their work was centered on *preaching* the kingdom. Only the prolonged delay of the Last Day, combined with speculation concerning the meaning of Jesus' words—factors that were at first attached to the preaching mission as defense against rival missionaries—open up the way for reflection and literary records.

SOCIAL FACTORS

A third factor bearing on the delay in producing narrative-accounts of the life of Jesus is the social composition of the early Christian churches. We do not know all that we would like to know about the early believers, but we do know enough to formulate a satisfactory picture of their position in society.[15] First we must dismiss the notion that Jesus himself was an educated man. The picture of him disputing with rabbis at the age of twelve, given only in Luke (2:46-48), is purely legendary and is intended to be a description of his divine powers (2:49), not his intellectual attainment. The fact that Jesus taught in the synagogue (Matt. 9:35; 4:23), according to tradition, should not be taken to mean that he was an expounder of religious truths. Indeed, references to this teaching show that his message was simply the coming kingdom. Further, the Gospels are transparently defensive about Jesus' synagogue-teaching and use it to counter the opinion—probably widespread among the Jewish opponents of Christianity—that Jesus had been an illiterate Nazarene.

On the occasion of his first synagogue appearance (Mark 6:1-3 and par.) the people are portrayed as being astonished that the son of a carpenter should be able to interpret scripture: "Where did this man get all this? What is the source of the wisdom given to Him?" Luke's rendering of this passage shows the christological tendency in bolder relief: first Jesus reads from Isaiah (61:1-2), "The spirit of the Lord is upon me," then announces, "Today this scripture has been fulfilled in your hearing." Instead of the people wondering about the source of his knowledge and taking offense at him (Mark 6:3), they are said to have spoken well of him and marvelled "at the gracious words which proceeded out of his mouth."

Here again, we have no reliable tradition concerning Jesus' educational achievement, but rather a story designed to show that the source of his wisdom was superior to that of the rabbis. Mark 6:3 is very telling on this point: it indicates that even the members of the synagogue in Nazareth, not the most cultivated of towns (see John 1:46), were offended at the sight of someone with this background teaching in public. Only Luke—and this later—invents the information that Jesus read "from a book," but in so doing he contradicts the information given by Mark and Matthew, to the effect that the townspeople of Nazareth regarded Jesus as a dilettante (Mark 6:4 ff.). It need hardly be said that Jesus' prospects in the more prosperous villages of Galilee, let alone Judea and in the city of Jerusalem, would have been worse than in his home town.

In each case, therefore, the Gospel picture of Jesus as an itinerant teacher (see Mark 1:21-28) is intended to emphasize his authority *in spite of* the fact that by contemporary standards he was considered unlettered and uncredentialed. Jesus belonged to a line of peripatetic preachers and would not have expected his message to be publicized in written form. Matthew preserves a plausible tradition (23:8) that Jesus withheld the respectful titles *rabbi* and *master,* both with implications of book-learning, from his followers; but the more intelligent reading of this verse is that contemporaries of the early missionaries regarded them as unworthy of such titles.

This leads us to consider the fact that Jesus did not choose scholars as disciples. Indeed, it is well known that apocalyptic enthusiasm did not flourish among the most enlightened circles in the middle of the first century, but rather among those depicted in the Gospels as the "lost sheep of the house of Israel" (Matt. 15.24): the poor, the diseased, and those who suffered most under the twin yokes of Rome and Jerusalem. The early Christians were in the habit of boasting that their movement was rooted among the poor and the ignorant. This is reflected in the Gospels by a prayer given to Jesus by Matthew and Luke, coming just after his "judgment" on the cities that had apparently rejected him and his message (Matt. 11:20). "At that time Jesus declared, 'I am grateful, Father, Lord of heaven and earth, that you have hidden these things from the wise and understanding and revealed them to babes; such was your gracious intention.'"

We read in this passage a reaction of the early missionaries to their own failures to persuade large numbers of people (those slightingly referred to as *sophoi* and *synetoi*—the intellectually well-formed) that the kingdom is at hand. The missionaries, remembering the rejection of their teacher, addressed themselves to the *ptōchoi tō pneumati,* the humble of mind ("poor in spirit"), the peacemakers, and the persecuted (Matt. 5:3-12). They would be the ones to benefit from the coming of the kingdom, the ones who, like the missionaries themselves, would be hated by the "wise," excluded from the synagogue, and reviled for holding to their conviction that the Son of Man was coming in judgment (Matt. 5:11 = Luke 6:22).

Clearly, the appeal of an apocalyptic message was not to the contented, but to the disenfranchised: such a message did not circulate in written form, since there were few who could have read it. Instead, believers carried it by word of mouth, working "signs" as evidence that the Last Days were fast approaching. Matthew 10 reflects the missionary practice of the early church, consisting of a series of "instructions" imagined to have come from Jesus. There we find that the missionaries were expected to live in poverty (in preparation for the Last Day), and to preach. As was the custom with wandering charismatics, the preachers expected to get subsistence from their listeners. (Matt. 10:10; Luke 10:7), but because of fear of persecution, had to be prepared for a getaway at all times (Matt. 10:23).

These wandering charismatics, the first founders of Christian "churches" (initially houses of Jesus-believers willing to feed and lodge the preachers), were intensely aware of their social and educational inferiority. They were suspicious of the ravenous "wolves," the Jewish intelligentsia who had rejected Jesus and his message (Matt. 10:16) and concerned that they would be tripped up in arguing in self-defense when hauled before sophisticated synagogue tribunals to answer for their opinions (10:19).

The Gospel emphasis on simplicity of heart and spirit, such as we find in the famous episode of Jesus blessing the little children (Matt. 19:13-15) has precious little to do with a concern for the welfare of the innocent; it is rather an indication of the pervasive anti-intellectualism of the Jesus-believers. The verse "For to such as these belong the Kingdom of Heaven" describes the attitude required for acceptance of the preaching. So, too, the parable of the laborers in the vineyard (Matt. 20), culminating in the verse "The last will be first and the first last" is the rhetoric of an oppressed group retrojecting into the teaching of the master their own conviction that they—not the wise or wealthy— would be inheritors of the kingdom when it came.

When one reads the Gospels carefully, this antagonism toward the rich (Matt. 19:22-24; 23:17) and the wise (Matt. 22:15; 23:1-11), and the contempt assigned to Jesus by the movement that "did not regard the position of men" (Matt. 22:16) is fairly clear. The believers made a virtue of the station imposed upon them by society (Matt. 23:11 = Mark 10:41-45), emphasizing brotherliness rather than learning. They rejoiced in the memory of a teacher who had often outwitted the Pharisees and left them speechless (Matt. 22:46), but they refused to be called "teachers" out of deference to his contempt for those who flaunted the title (Matt. 23:8).

It is obvious therefore that both Jesus and his followers were wandering preachers who attracted small numbers of local sympathizers (thus the house of Lazarus in Bethany), but because of the nature of their message and their lack of skill in disputing with the teachers (in marked contrast to the believers' memory of affairs) were unable to mobilize great numbers.

If we imagine this to have been the situation in the 30s and 40s, it is no wonder that a written "gospel" or some other transcript of Jesus' sayings and deeds was not produced. During these years, the message remained essentially the message preached *by* Jesus combined with further declarations, themselves slow to take specific form, about his conquest of death (see Acts 2:22-36) and "elevation" to messianic status by God. In Paul's first letter to the Corinthians, written in the 50s of the first century, we find the social situation scarcely changed, even though the coming of the kingdom—the core of Jesus' preaching—has been supplanted by preaching about the "Christ."

Christ did not send me to baptize but to preach the gospel, and not with eloquent wisdom lest the cross of Christ be emptied of its power . . . [1 Cor. 1:17]

It is written, "I will destroy the wisdom of the wise, and the cleverness of the clever I will thwart." Where is this wise man? Where is the scribe? Where is the debater of this age? Has God not made foolish the wisdom of the world! [1 Cor. 1:19-20]

Consider your call, brethren, not many of you were wise according to worldly standards, not many were powerful, not many of noble birth; but God chose the foolish in the world to shame the wise. [1 Cor. 1:26]

We cannot analyze the local problems of the church at Corinth which provoke Paul to write this letter of reproof. We can say that its main cause is a kind of gnostic heresy that Paul sees infecting an otherwise undistinguished group of believers, or some portion of them, with the opinion that they possess a special gift of spiritual wisdom *(gnosis/ sophia)*. Paul thus writes to remind the congregation that by the standards obtaining in the outside world, they are unlearned and foolish; that the only wisdom they can lay claim to is having accepted his "absurd" gospel of a crucified Christ (1 Cor. 1:22), a message thought scandalous by the Jews and incomprehensible by Gentiles.

Paul's contempt for "human" standards of wisdom and authority is deep-seated: His unsystematic theology, arising mainly from self-defensive diatribes against rival preachers, is characterized by a dislike of learning and philosophy that blends ill with the legend that he was a pupil of the famous Rabbi Gamaliel. "My speech and my message were not in plausible words of wisdom, but in demonstration of the Spirit and of power, so that your faith might not rest in the wisdom of men" (1 Cor. 2:4-5). But though Paul's own learning must be called into question on the basis of such confessions (he "marked" but did not write his letters: see 1 Cor. 16:21; Rom. 16:22), he heartily disapproved of the spectacle—perhaps widespread among gnostic Christian communities—of the equally untutored boasting of "superior" wisdom and spiritual gifts surpassing those of the educated.

We need only mention in passing that the phenomenon described in 1 Corinthians 12-14, a spectacle which greatly exercises Paul (and perplexes a good many people today) is the most unlikely inheritance of primitive Christianity: *glossolalia* (speaking in tongues). The practice is nevertheless a clue to determining the educational accomplishment of the Christians at Corinth. The practice then as now was dearest to those who, through a sense of intellectual inferiority combined with a natural inclination toward emotional display, considered these tongues of ecstasy to be proof of some high spiritual endowment—a "learning" exceeding that of the wise. Paul is gentle, but not uncritical of the babbling contests that threaten to displace the gospel in Corinth (1 Cor. 14:2-4). Apparently, the congregation included—perhaps among some better elements—reformed robbers, sexual perverts, and drunkards (1 Cor. 6:9-11).

The social situation of the Christian churches had scarcely changed by the end of the second century when the philosopher Celsus, in his diatribe against the obscurantism of the Christians, reported:

> [Christians] do not even want to give or to receive a reason for what they believe, and use such expressions as "Do not ask questions; just believe" and "Thy faith will save thee." . . . Their injunctions are like this: "Let no one educated, no one wise, no one sensible draw near. For these abilities are thought by us to be evil. But as for anyone ignorant, anyone stupid, anyone uneducated, anyone who is a child, let him come boldly." By the fact that they themselves admit that these people are worthy of their God, they show that they want and are able to convince only the foolish, dishonourable, and stupid, and only slaves, women, and little children . . . . In private houses also we see wool-workers, cobblers, laundry workers, and the most bucolic and illiterate yokels, who would not dare to say anything at all in front of their elders and more intelligent masters.[16]

Even the opponents of Christianity bear witness to the fact that the primary targets of the missionary preaching were those who could apprehend the gospel only in oral form. Although written gospels certainly existed in Celsus' day, they existed to be *preached* by presbyters able to read and interpret the text of scriptures.

DOCTRINE

Finally, it must be pointed out that Paul—and thus his congregations—knows almost no historical tradition *about* Jesus, beyond the
mere "facts" of his birth, passion, crucifixion, and resurrection (see 1
Cor. 11:23; 15:3-7). For Paul, Jesus is first and foremost the Christ:
"Even though we once regarded Christ from the human point of view,
we regard him thus no longer" (2 Cor. 5:16). This transformation of
the historical Jesus into the cultic Christ is reflected in even the earliest
of Paul's letters. One must be aware, therefore, that the progressive
tendency to regard Jesus as a divine being—the Son of God—from an
early date resulted in comparative disinterest in the facts of his life and
the substance of his teaching. Paul's preaching clearly reflects this lack
of interest. Obviously, when the gospel-tradition finally acquires written form, *it does so under the influence of specific doctrines about
Jesus as the Christ,* and not out of any purely historical interest in
preserving the facts of his existence. But it is fair to say that if this
transformation had not taken place, there would have been no recovery
of interest in the Jesus who had lived and taught in Galilee and was
crucified according to Roman law. It is precisely his *posthumous* (and
not his contemporary) significance and the need to communicate this
to later generations—generations never envisioned by Jesus or those
who had heard him—that leads to the gathering and stitching together
of the "gospels."

How many of these there were, we cannot know; but the prologue
to Luke suggests there was a great variety in circulation toward the
close of the first century. Many more were written in the second century. The extant Gospels were written as retrospectives of a life from
which most—though not all—of the biographical facts have been ex-
tricated and replaced by the beliefs, defenses, or opinions of the early
church, a fact which makes a rich storehouse of information about the
development of Christianity, but a less than satisfactory account of the
life and teaching of Jesus.

Three

JESUS OUTSIDE THE GOSPELS

This brings us to the work at hand. What is known of Jesus *outside* the Gospels? Are such materials any more useful for reconstructing his life and teaching than the Gospels themselves? Do any noncanonical sources exist that are *older* than the canonical Gospels—sources to which the Gospels themselves might (in various ways) be indebted?

There are, of course, many good reasons for desiring such sources. The impartial student of history will have the same interest in knowing whether Jesus existed as in knowing whether Alexander the Great or Homer really lived. It is not enough simply to be able to take the measure of such figures by the ripples they have made in the stream of history; for many, it is important to know something about the size, color, and shape of the person responsible for the disturbance.

For others, the existence of Jesus and the events of his life have a further dimension, rooted in their belief that God made his will and purpose manifest in a unique historical individual. Such people will normally see extra-Gospel sources as supplementing, but not necessarily establishing, a conclusion they base primarily on the literature produced by the Christian movement itself. An obvious problem with this approach—one too often neglected by those Christians who have confused "Bible study" with scholarship—is that the Gospels were not intended to establish the *historicity* of Jesus but rather his *divinity*. While they remain the fullest account of his life and teaching, they present this teaching within a theological framework that makes them unsuitable for use as straightforward, documentary evidence. They also embody a mythological view of the world—a three-storied cosmos with a flat earth ruled over by demons who delight in taking up temporary residence in the minds and bodies of innocent victims—that began to crumble in the sixteenth century. Further, we must be prepared to acknowledge that Jesus, far from being the omniscient Son of God who reads the hearts and minds of men, *shared* the world-view of his contemporaries.

Finally, there are those who will want to have outside sources in order to make up their minds about the Gospels. This is perhaps the most "reasonable" approach of the three, since the sources are not early enough to satisfy the historian, nor impressive enough to provide additional support for the believer's view of the Gospel record. The Jesus-tradition did not grow up *within* the New Testament canon; the New Testament canon represents rather a decision—not unambiguous or early—about what parts of this tradition deserve credit, and what parts supported Christian teaching. The orthodox Jesus-tradition represented in the Gospels grows up in tension with heresy: apocryphal gospels and epistles that offer "alternative" (not always minority) opinions about Jesus and what he taught; Jewish polemic that contradicts central elements of the Gospel story; and pagan opinion about the beliefs and practices of the early Jesus-believers.

The New Testament canon, the twenty-seven books revered by many today as divine revelation, is actually only the authorized portrait of Jesus of Nazareth, a portrait painstakingly but not altogether consistently produced by the church that claimed him as its founder. In order to evaluate this portrait thoughtfully, one must take into account the several kinds of material provided in this collection, attentive to the fact that any conclusion based on the Gospels alone is bound to be incomplete and uninformed.

Jewish Sources

INTRODUCTION

Voltaire presents the following dialogue between a rationalist believer and a doubter in his *Dialogues satiriques:*

BELIEVER: The Jews are the crudest of Asiatics . . . Their historical traditions are utterly foolish and futile.
DOUBTER: Nonetheless, Jesus, whom you love, was a Jew. He always observed the Jewish religion and adhered to its customs.

Perplexed, the BELIEVER answers: This is a great contradiction; for though he was a Jew, his followers were not Jews. [Sat. XI]

The matter was not so perplexing for the German scholar Hermann Samuel Reimarus, who wrote in 1767:

I cannot avoid revealing a common error of Christians, who imagine because of the confusion of the teaching of the apostles with Jesus' teaching that the latter's purpose . . . was to reveal certain articles of faith and mysteries that were in part new and unknown, thus establishing a new system of religion [and] doing away with the Jewish religion in regard to its special customs, such as sacrifices, circumcision, purification, the Sabbath, and other Levitical ceremonies. . . . [Jesus] was born a Jew and intended to remain one. . . . He proposed no new mysteries or articles of faith and had no intention of doing away with [Jewish] ceremonial law.[1]

New Testament scholars have long since accepted these eighteenth-century recognitions: Jesus was born, lived, and died a Jew. His outlook was in large part determined by the synagogue Judaism of his day, and even his attempted "reformation" of Jewish law is more clearly seen from within the context of first-century Judaism than outside it.

Since Jesus conducted his own ministry exclusively on Jewish soil (a fact often overlooked), it is appropriate to turn first to the Jewish sources concerning his life and teaching. These sources will be unfamiliar to many, and require some introduction. They occur chiefly in two places: the Talmud, a massive compilation embodying the *Mishnah* (oral teaching) and the *Gemara* (collections of discussions on the Mishnah), formed during the fifth century CE;[2] and in *Midrash* (Heb: investigation), scriptural exegesis and exposition, containing *Hag-*

gadah (edifying sermons and folklore, as also found in Gemara and rabbinical writings) and *Halakha* (legally binding decisions derived from the Torah by rabbinical logic). Midrash originated in the period of the *Soferim* or scribes, of which Ezra (fourth century BC) is reputed to have been the first. The earliest collections of Midrashim do not date from before the second century CE, though much of the traditional material is considerably older. These collections are of great importance for the light they shed on the Jewish belief and practice of Jesus' day.

Jesus lived in the era of the great rabbinical schools: Rabbis Hillel (flourished about 70), the father of a liberal and conciliatory Judaism, Shammai (fl. c. 40), the champion of Jewish fundamentalism, and Gamaliel ("who had a reputation among all peoples," Acts 5:34) were his near contemporaries. It might be expected, therefore, that the "Sages of the Talmud" would have a great deal to say about Jesus of Nazareth. But this is not the case. In the first place, the Talmud authorities rarely refer to the events of the period of the Second Temple (that is, the structure rededicated under Judas Maccabeus in 164 BC, following its desecration in 168 by the Syrians), which includes the period up to the Roman conquest of Jerusalem in 70 AD. This, almost unfortunately, encompasses the years Jesus is thought to have lived.

Second, the appearance of Jesus during the period of turmoil which befell Judea under the Herods and Roman procurators was a relatively inconspicuous event, hardly noticed by his contemporaries. By the time Christianity became powerful enough to be noticed, popular stories and legends about Jesus—some known even to pagan philosophers such as Celsus—had filled the void where memory failed. The Talmud references to Jesus, therefore, contain many legends that are known to us from the Gospels—but are given a decidedly anti-Christian twist. For example, the Gospels say that Jesus was born of the Holy Spirit and not of a human father; the Talmud stories assert that he was indeed born without a legitimate father—as the result of an illicit liaison between his mother and a Roman soldier. The Gospels say that Jesus worked miracles as signs of his messianic status and through the power of God; the Talmud stories know him as a sorcerer and magician. Finally, in the Gospels Jesus is portrayed as an opponent of the scribes and Pharisees with their "rote-learned precepts" and as a friend of sinners. The Jewish sources—unsurprisingly—maintain that Jesus was a "sinner in Israel" and a "scoffer against the words of the wise." *Nevertheless, the earliest of the Talmud sources date from a time well before the latest of the Gospels reached its final form, and one cannot exclude the possibility that many stories in the Gospels are specific responses to the Jewish picture of Jesus given in the Talmud.* Instances of this will be given in due course.

A third and final reason for the scarcity of the references to Jesus in the Talmud must be attributed to the Christian church. From the time of Justin Martyr (fl. 160) on, Christianity found itself in a continuous and often bitter conversation with Judaism. By the ninth century, references to the "foul and perfidious Jews" had become a fixed part of the Good Friday liturgy of the Western rite, an attitude that marks the transition from disapproval of those Jews who (according to Christian legend) had conspired to kill Jesus and a wholesale anti-Semitism that infected all of Europe. One aspect of Christian intolerance was papal censorship of the Talmud and Midrash: What survived the ink of zealous censors was partially restored from miscellaneous manuscripts in 1900 by Professor G. Dalman in a monograph entitled *Die Thalmudischen Texte Über Jesu* (Talmudic Texts Concerning Jesus), but it is certain that many more references have been lost.

We can derive from the remaining sources what the Sages of Israel thought of the origin and teaching of Jesus some seventy years or so after he was crucified and the reasons for his unpopularity among the teachers of the Law.

This view can be summarized as follows: Yeshu (Hebrew, Joshua) of Nazareth practiced sorcery and led people astray from Jewish doctrine by his teaching; he was a trickster and a heretic who mocked the words of the Pharisees. He had five disciples who constituted a *minim* or sect within Judaism and who healed the sick in his name. He taught (deceptively) that he had not come to add to or take away from the Law. He was hanged (crucified?) on the eve of Passover as a heretic. Other statements, chiefly but not exclusively of a polemical nature, suggest that he was the bastard son of an adulteress (the hairdresser, Miriam) and a Roman father named Pandera or Panthere; that for forty days before his execution a herald was sent out looking for those who would plead in his favor but could find no one to do so; that the rabbis of his generation taught that this Yeshu would have no share in the world to come.

These polemical statements were long-lived and known to Celsus, who comments on the illegitimacy of Jesus and the absurdity of the story of the virgin birth (Origen, *Contra Celsum* 1.9.1). Undoubtedly, the bulk of this Jewish tradition can be traced back to a period before the formation of the written Gospels. Some passages in the Gospels— such as Matthew 27:62-66 (the posting of a guard outside the tomb) show the clear imprint of Christian counterpolemic against the Jewish charge prevalent throughout the first century—that Jesus' disciples had stolen his body and then declared him risen from the dead. So too, the story of the flight into Egypt (Matt. 2:13-15), which the author of the first Gospel strains to relate to an Old Testament prophecy (the slaughter of infants reported by Matthew is legendary), is perhaps a response to the Talmudic charge that Jesus had learned magic and sorcery in Egypt. Such passages illustrate the importance of reading the rabbinical references carefully, as possible precipitants of Gospel accounts. The excerpts below are followed by short commentaries.

THE BIRTH OF JESUS

> Rabbi Eliezer said to the sages, "Did not Ben Stada bring spells from Egypt in a cut on his flesh?" They replied, "He was a fool and one does not prove anything from a fool." Ben Stada is Ben Pandira. Rabbi Hisda [a Babylonian teacher of the third century] said, "The husband was Stada, the paramour was Pandira." The husband was Pappos ben Jehudah, the mother was Stada. The mother was Miriam, the dresser of women's hair—as we say in Pumbeditha [a Babylonian town where there was a famous rabbinical college], "Such a one has been false to her husband." [Shabbath 104[b]][3]

This passage occurs in a Mishnah discussion concerning the propriety of writing on the Sabbath. In the course of discussion, the question of writing or marking on the flesh is introduced: Rabbi Eliezer suggests that as (Yeshu) ben Stada has brought spells from Egypt, the practice may be permissible. To this Rabbi Hisda replies that Ben Stada, also known as Ben Pandira, was a fool, and his case proves nothing.

There is considerable confusion in the Gemara about parentage: Stada is first (mistakenly) said to be the name of the paramour; but the name derives from the phrase *S'tath da* (lit., "she went astray"), so that Stada is actually an epithetic name for the mother, the real father being Pandira, and the husband of Miriam being Pappos ben Jehudah. Thus, the two names being discussed by the rabbis, *Ben Stada* (son of one who went astray) and *Ben Pandira* (son of Panther) refer to the same person. That this person is Jesus of Nazareth is clear from the fact that we elsewhere meet with the full name, Jeshu ben Pandira and Jeshu ben Stada.[4]

There are a number of points of contact between Gospel tradition and the preceding passage. We have already commented on the parallel between the Matthean story of a journey into Egypt soon after Jesus' birth (Matt. 2:13) and the rabbis' belief that Jesus learned magical arts there. Also to be noticed is the tradition that Jesus' mother was named Mary (= Miriam) and that her husband was not the father of Jesus (see Mark 6:3; Luke 3:23). The Gospel-accounts attributed to Matthew and Luke attempt to overcome this apparently well-known accusation with contradictory stories about a virgin birth. Matthew 1:18-25 clearly preserves and reflects the rabbinical story concerning Jesus' illegitimacy. Concerning the idea that Mary was a dresser of women's hair we can only speculate: the cult of Mary in the Middle Ages destroyed all historical traditions concerning her life, and belief in her immaculate conception is already implicit in the *Book of James* (pp. 105-116).

Perhaps the rabbis confused Miriam and the sinner Mary Magdalene (Luke 7:37-8:2; Mark 15:40; Matt 28:9), about whom even the Gospels offer confused reports. The "floating" tradition concerning the woman taken in adultery (John 7:53-8:11), if part of the Mary-tradition, may point to an early stratum when Mary the mother of Jesus and Mary of Magdala were one and the same. In any case, the Gospel tradition concerning the latter Mary may have emerged as a corrective to the story that Jesus' mother was an adulteress. The probability of this is increased since the phrase "dresser of women's hair" in the Talmud reads *Miriam, m'gadella nashaia.*

Origins of the tradition concerning the "two fathers" of Yeshu are more difficult to determine. The most plausible explanation of the name Ben Pandira (Pandera, Pantira) is that the Greek *panthera* (panther) was a pun on the Christian belief that Jesus was the son of a virgin (Greek, *parthenos*). Why a Greek word should have been chosen as an epithet for Jesus is unclear, however, and since the pun is such a poor one we cannot rule out the possibility that there is a kernel of historical truth to the tradition that Jesus' real father was known as Pandira. We are in a better position to disqualify Pappos ben Jehudah as the husband of Miriam. This legendary figure is thought to have lived a century *after* Jesus in the time of Rabbi Aqiba. His renown comes from the story that he was so jealous of his wife that he locked her in the house whenever he went out. But this anachronism does not prove the Gospel tradition concerning Joseph's espousal of Mary to be accurate: the doctrine of virgin birth nullifies the two different Davidic genealogies in Matt 1:1-17 and Luke 3:23-34 and makes Joseph merely the foster father of Jesus; further, the earliest Gospel, Mark, does not appear to know any tradition concerning Jesus' true father (6:2-4).

> When Rabbi Joseph came to this verse [Exod. 23:17] he wept . . . . He said, "Is there any who has departed before his time? None but this [as told of] Rab Bibi bar Aboji." The angel of death was with him. The angel said to his messenger, "Go, bring me Miriam, the dresser of women's hair." He brought him Miriam the teacher of children [by mistake]. [The angel] said, "I told thee Miriam, the dresser of women's hair." He said, "If so, I will take this one back." He said, "Since you have brought this one, let her remain among [the dead]."
>
> The angel of death was with him: he related what had already happened, for this about Miriam the dresser of women's hair took place in the time of the second Temple, for she was the mother of a certain person. [Hag. 4[b] and Tosaphoth]

This passage and the personages named in it belong to late third-century Babylon: Rabbi Joseph was head of the college at Pumbe-ditha. The passage does not add much to our knowledge of rabbinical opinion about Jesus or his parentage, though it does suggest that the Miriam-tradition was known in the Babylonian schools at the end of the third century.

> Rabbi Shimon ben 'Azai said, "I have found a roll of pedigrees in Jerusalem where it is written, a certain person was born a bastard of an adulteress confirming the words of Rabbi Jehoshua." [M. Jeb. 4.13]

This passage belongs to the older stratum of the Talmud: Rabbi ben Azai was a contemporary of Aqiba at the end of the first century, and both were students of Rabbi Jehoshua. The latter's teacher, Rabbi ben Zacchai, could have seen and remembered Jesus. Both Aqiba and Jehoshua were ardent opponents of the Minim, the heretical sect of Jews who had proclaimed the messiahship of Jesus. The charge of Jesus' illegitimacy is here emphasized by reference to a "book of pedigrees" that lists Jesus as a *mamzer*, a person of spurious birth. Herford, in *Christianity in Talmud and Midrash* (p. 45), holds it possible that such a book existed prior to 135. The contrived genealogy in Matthew 1:1-17 may be an answer to Ben Azai's claim to have seen documentary proof of Jesus' illegitimacy.

> Rabbi Johanan said [of Balaam], "In the beginning a prophet, in the end, a deceiver." Rabbi Papa said, "This is the one of whom they say, 'She was the descendant of princes and rulers, she played the harlot with carpenters.'" [b. Sanh. 106ª]

The reference to Balaam in this excerpt is a covert reference to Jesus. Otherwise, the passage is clearly a slur against the mother of Jesus. In Matthew 13:55, Jesus is called "the carpenter's son" (the carpenter being unnamed) in a pejorative context; the verse carries the implication that his mother and the carpenter were not married. The redaction of this verse from Mark 6:3 (see Luke 4:22) is a complicated question in New Testament exegesis, but the legend of Jesus being the son of a kindly Nazarene carpenter named Joseph may well derive from rabbin-

ical slurs, such as this relatively late one (c. fourth century). It is clear
even from the Gospels that the tradition concerning Jesus' mother is
far more secure than any identification of his father (see Mark 3:31-35
and pars.). Later pious contrivances concerning the extreme age of
Joseph at the time of his betrothal to Mary do not disguise the fact
that outside the early chapters of the Gospels of Luke and Matthew,
where he is introduced largely as a convenience, he plays no role at all.

THE LIFE OF JESUS

> When Jannai the King killed our rabbis, R. Jehoshua ben Perabjah and
> Jeshu fled to Alexandria of Egypt. When there was peace, Shimon ben
> Shetah sent to him, "From [Jerusalem] the city of holiness to thee
> Alexandria of Egypt: my husband stays in thy midst and I sit forsaken."
> He came and found himself at a certain inn; they showed him great
> honor. He said, "How beautiful is this inn." Jesus said to him, "Rabbi
> [the hostess] has narrow eyes!" He said, "Fool, do you pay attention to
> such things." He sent out four hundred trumpets and cast him out. Jesus
> came before him many times thereafter, pleading, "Receive me back."
> But Jehoshua did not receive him. One day R. Jehoshua was saying
> Shema and Jesus came before him. R. Jehoshua signalled that he would
> receive Jesus, but Jesus thought that the rabbi repelled him. Then Jesus
> went out and hung up a tile and worshipped it. R. Jehoshua said to him,
> "Return [to the teaching of your fathers]" but Jesus said, "I have learned
> from you that everyone who sins and causes others to sin is given no
> chance to repent." Thus a teacher had said, Jesus the Nazarene practiced
> magic and led astray and deceived Israel. [b. Sanh. 107ᵇ]

The significance of this passage is twofold. On the one hand, it
presents Jesus as a heretic who departs from the learning of his teacher
and goes on to preach heresy *(minuth)* in Israel. More problematical is
the dating of Jesus' heresy: Here the Talmud pictures Jesus as active
during the reign of "Jannai the King," that is, Alexander Jannaeus, who
reigned from 104 to 78 BC. Jehoshua ben Perabjah (Jehudah ben
Tabbai in the Palestinian version) was a leading Pharisee of the time,
and the slaughter of the rabbis mentioned in the opening verses is an

historical event. Possibly, the story has links with the Gospel account of a flight into Egypt to avoid the anger of a king (Matt. 2:13 f.). It also preserves a recollection of Jesus setting himself against the authority of the rabbis, though the commoner association of Jesus and Rabbi Eliezer is missing. The polemical thrust of the passage is difficult to overlook: Jesus is here presented not only as a rebellious disciple but as an idolator (that is, one who worships tiles or burned bricks) and one who causes multitudes to sin. The story probably originated in Palestine close to the time Jesus actually lived, but makes use of an anachronism to make its polemical point.

"He that cuts marks on his flesh," Rabbi Eliezer condemns, the wise permit. He said to them, "Did not Yeshu ben Stada learn only in this way?" They said to him "Because of one fool, are we to destroy all discerning people?" [T. Shabb. 11.15]

In a similar passage (j. Shabb. 13^d) the rabbis' discussion centers on Jesus' parentage. Here, the emphasis is on Jesus' reputation as a magician. The Talmud knows Egypt as the center of the magical arts: "Ten measures of sorcery descended into the world: Egypt received nine, the rest of the world one" (Talmud b. Qidd. 49^b). Thus, to say that Jesus learned magic in Egypt is to say that he is more powerful as a worker of signs than the local variety of wonder-workers (see Matt. 9:33).

"There shall no evil befall thee." This means that evil dreams and evil thoughts will not tempt you; "neither shall any plague come near thy dwelling" (Ps. 91:10) means that you will not have a son or disciple who burns his food in public like Jesus of Nazareth. [b. Sanh. 103^a]

This obscure passage, dating from the fourth century, contains the apparently damaging charge that Jesus burned his food in public. The phrase is idiomatic and means "brings himself into disrepute."[5] It was especially applied to those who were suspected of heresy; thus the appellation to Jesus.

Rabbi Abahu said, "If a man says to you, I am God, he is a liar. If he says, I am the Son of Man, people will, in the end, laugh at him. And if he says, I will go up to heaven, he will not carry it out, though he say it." [j. Taanith 65^b]

This attack on the central doctrines of Christian belief dates from around the third century. The speaker, Rabbi Abahu, lived in Caesarea, and was accustomed to dealing with Jewish heretics of various stripes, including Christians. The haggadah he offers is based on Numbers 23:19—"God is not a man that he should lie, nor the son of man that he should repent." A similar attack on the Christian "heresy" of the divinity of Jesus follows:

He looked forth and beheld that there was a man, son of a woman, who should rise up and seek to make himself God and to cause the whole world to go astray. [Jalq. Shim. Paragraph 766]

This passage incorporates the substance of the charge brought against Jesus by the Jewish council (Luke 22:66-71), though the information that "he has caused the whole world to go astray" points to a date of composition well into the third century. Rabbi El'zaar ha-Qappar, who is credited with the saying, died about 260 AD.

Three kings and four private persons have no part in the world to come: the kings are Jeroboam, Ahab and Manasseh; the others are Balaam, Doeg, Ahitophel and Gehazi. [M. Sanh. X.2]

The persons denied a part in the world to come include Jesus, here under the familiar name of Balaam (see Num. 22). In the paragraph immediately preceding this extract, the excluded are said to be "those who say the resurrection of the dead is not proved from Torah and that the Torah is not from heaven," a clear reference to the Christians who were reckoned—against Gospel testimony of a gratuitous character (Matt. 5:17)—to have rejected the Law and not to base their belief in the resurrection on the Torah. From the Jewish point of view, there was considerable likeness between Jesus and Balaam: both had led the people astray; the former had tempted them to immorality, the latter to apostasy and betrayal of the covenant.

Onqelos . . . desired to become a Jew. . . . He called up Balaam by
sorcery and said to him, "Who is honored in the world?" [Balaam]
replied, "Israel." "What about joining them?" He answered, "You shall
not seek their peace or their prosperity all your days. . . ."
   He called up Jesus by sorcery and said to him: "Who is honored in
this world?" He answered, "Israel." "What about joining them?" He
answered, "Seek their good, seek not their harm. Everyone who injures
them, it is as if he injured the apple of his eye." He said, "What is the
punishment of this man?" He replied, "By boiling filth . . . for a teacher
has said, "Everyone who mocks at the words of the wise is punished by
boiling filth." Come and see the difference between the sinners of Israel
and those who serve false religion. [b. Gitt 56ᵇ, 57ᵃ]

   This extract is part of a long Midrash describing the punishment
of the enemies of Israel's religion: Titus, Balaam, and Jesus are con-
jured up in succession, and each describes the fate awaiting the non-
believer or transgressor. Older editions of the Talmud expunged Jesus'
name. He is remembered here as one who "mocked the words of the
wise," a theme familiar from the Gospels (Matt. 5:20; 15:7, 12).

   A certain heretic said to Rabbi Hanina, "Have you ever heard how old
   Balaam [= Jesus] was?" He replied, "There is nothing written about it.
   But from what is written (Ps. 55:23), 'Men of blood and deceit live out
   half their days,' he must have been thirty-three or thirty-four years old."
   [b. Sanh. 106ᵇ]

   Rabbi Hanina lived in Sepphoris at the end of the second century.
The information he offers to the heretic (probably an inquisitive Christian)
is unparalleled in the Gospels. Luke 3:23 specifies that Jesus was about
thirty years old when he began his work (the traditional age of a
teacher); but no Gospel reports his age at the time of the crucifixion.
The Synoptics imply a one-year ministry; the Gospel of John, a ministry covering at least three. Further in the same passage, the heretic
speaks of a "chronicle of Balaam," perhaps a reference to a Gospel.
The heretic and the rabbi—significantly—do not disagree over the age
of Jesus, though the latter finds "proof" in the psalm that he was a
deceiver.

THE TRIAL OF JESUS

> In regard to all who are worthy of death according to the Torah, they
> do not use concealment against them except in the case of the deceiver.
> How do they deal with him? They put two disciples of the wise in the
> inner chamber, and he sits in the outer chamber, and they light the lamp
> so that they shall see him and hear his voice. And thus they did to Jeshu
> ben Stada in Lūd; two disciples of the wise were chosen for him, and
> they brought him to the Beth Din and stoned him. [T. Sanh. X.11 and
> with variations, J. Sanh. 7.16. (25^{c,d})]

The following passage elaborates the legal proceedings used in the
case of a "deceiver."

> They light a lamp for him in the inner chamber and set witnesses in the
> outer chamber so that they may see him and hear his voice, but he does
> not see them. And one says to him, "Say to me what you said to me in
> private," and he says it to him. And another says to him, "How shall we
> forsake our God who is in heaven and practice false worship?" If [the
> deceiver] repents, it is well. If he says, "Such is our duty; we must do as I
> have taught," the witnesses who hear from the outside bring him to the
> Beth Din [House of Judgment, often used to denote a tribunal of
> rabbis] and stone him. And thus they did to Yeshu ben Stada in Lūd,
> and they hung him on the eve of Pesah [Passover].

The preceding passages outline the procedures used in the case of
those who tempt others into apostasy. Entrapment of the accused,
according to Mishnah, was reserved for such cases. Moreover, we are
confronted here with a precedent that contradicts the Gospel accounts
of the trial and execution of Jesus. Coming as it does from Jewish
sources, it cannot be overlooked, since Christian polemic against the
Jews strove hard to implicate them in Jesus' death (Mark 14:55, pars.).
The Gospel story of the trial of Jesus is so filled with inaccuracies,
however, that it cannot be held inherently more credible than the
rabbinical accounts, which remember the trial of Jesus to have been a
strictly *internal* affair, and his punishment for heresy stoning rather

than crucifixion—the latter normally used only by the Romans.

It should be recognized that the early Jesus-believers, motivated by apologetic and political concerns, would have repelled the suggestion that their master had been sentenced and executed by his own kinsmen, as they would later be embarrassed by the *opposite* claim—and seek to mitigate it (John 9:12); namely, that a Roman procurator was responsible for the death of Jesus. The unhappy compromise—reflected in the panoply of trials, accusations, and decisions—is that while the Jews conspired to kill Jesus, brought the charges, and insisted on his death (Mark 15:8-15), they did not actually carry out the sentence. The author of 1 Thessalonians 2:14-15 seems to know a different tradition. It should also be stressed that the Talmudic literature is absolutely silent concerning any Roman part in the trial and execution of Ben Stada—a fact difficult to explain in view of the Christian willingness to (partially) exculpate the Jews. The consistency of the Talmud on this point should not be overlooked. So too with the name of the place of execution, Lūd (or Lydda), the method of execution (stoning), and in the last passage, the time: the eve of Passover. The following extract provides a fuller view of the execution:

> According to tradition, they hung Jeshu the Nazarene on the Eve of Passover. A crier went out forty days before saying, "Jeshu the Nazarene is going to be stoned because he has practiced magic and led Israel astray. If anyone can speak in his favor, let him come forth and declare himself." But they found no one to do so. And they hung him on the eve of Passover. Ulla says, "Would it be supposed that Jeshu, a revolutionary, had something in his favor?" He was a deceiver—and the merciful has said "You shall not spare nor hide such a one." But it was different with Jeshu the Nazarene, for he was near the kingdom. [b. Sanh. 43ᵃ]

It has been argued that the substitution of Lūd for Jerusalem in these accounts is due to the fact that following the destruction of Jerusalem, Lydda became the most important center of rabbinical activity: Eliezer, Tarphon, and Aqiba, all renowned for their learning, kept schools there. Lūd was also a headquarters for insurgent activity during the Bar Cochba revolt (132-135), and the name "martyrs of Lydda" was bestowed on the rabbis who were killed in the insurrection. Apparently, the writers of this passage think of Jesus as both an insurgent and an apostate, who nonetheless remained faithful to his calling ("He was near the kingdom"). The writer also thinks of Jesus as a contemporary of Aqiba, and doubtless knows of tensions between Christians and Jews in Lydda, Christians refusing to acknowledge Bar Cochba as Messiah (Justin, *Apol.* 1.100.31).

Thus, the historical context into which Jesus' execution is placed is mistaken, but some memory of his revolutionary activities may be preserved. The information that Jesus was hung is not, as such, a contradiction of the information that he was stoned on the eve of Passover; from Mishnah, Sanh. 6.4, Rabbi Eliezer points out that "all who are stoned are hung," so that the dead body of Jesus would have been put on display following his execution. This humiliation, according to the same text (a gloss of Deut. 21:23) was reserved for "the blasphemer and those who practice false worship." Such, according to the tradition preserved in the Gospel, was the accusation of the chief priest (Mark 14:63). The information that no one could be found to testify in Jesus' favor tallies roughly with the Gospel story of the desertion of the apostles and Peter's denial (Mark 14:66-72).

THE TOL'DOTH JESHU[6]

The *Tol'doth Jeshu,* in part from the fifth century, weaves together early and late Talmudic and Midrashic legends and sayings concerning Jesus. Many of the accounts incorporated in the *Tol'doth Jeshu* date from the second century or earlier, since there are references to such a collection of stories in the writings of the church fathers, Origen and Tertullian. In the ninth century, a copy of the book fell into the hands of Agobard, bishop of Lyons, who wrote a diatribe against it entitled, "De judaicis superstitionibus" (Concerning Jewish Superstitions). In 1902, Samuel Krauss gathered together a number of Aramaic fragments of disparaging stories about Jesus *(Das Leben Jesu nach jüdischen Quellen,* pp. 181-194), which testify to the existence of an early date for individual parts of the material contained in the *Tol'doth*

Jeshu. Other scholars, like Joseph Klausner,[7] would argue for a late date of composition (not before the tenth century) and on this reckoning challenge its historical value. However, the mere fact that the stories are disparaging and legendary is not sufficient to support the idea that they were *composed* a long time after the written Gospels. Furthermore, the *Tol'doth Jeshu* differs from the Gospel accounts in so many respects that the theory of literary dependence of the former on the latter must be rejected.

A certain man named Yochanan who was learned in the Law and feared God, a man of the House of David, was betrothed to a virgin of humble birth named Miriam, the daughter of his widowed neighbor. This was in Bethlehem. Miriam, however, was seduced by a handsome fellow named Joseph ben Pondera, who tricked her on a Sabbath eve [in the following manner]: Miriam had thought that [Pondera] was her espoused husband, Yochanan, and submitting only against her will, was astonished that her husband-to-be would act in such a way. When [the real] Yochanan returned she chastised him for his behavior. [Yochanan] suspected Pondera and reported these suspicions to Rabbi Shimeon ben Shesah. When it was known that Miriam was pregnant, Yochanan knew that it was not his; but unable to prove the guilt of [Pondera], he fled to Babylon.

Miriam brought forth a son and called him Yehoshua after her mother's brother. This name, in due course, was shortened to Yeshu. The child learned the Law from an able teacher and scholar—but in the long run, proved independent and precocious. On one occasion, he passed in front of the teachers with his head uncovered, whereupon the teachers rebuked him as a bastard and a child of impunity. Miriam confessed to this, whereupon Shimeon ben Shesah recalled what Yochanan had told him.

Yeshu fled to Jerusalem. In the Temple he learned the Ineffable Name. And to thwart the brass dogs who guarded the place of sacrifice and barked at those who had learned the name, making them forget, Yeshu wrote the name on a piece of leather and sewed it in the flesh of his thigh. He gathered around him in Bethlehem a group of young Jews and proclaimed himself the Messiah and Son of God. He rebuked those who rejected his claim, saying that they were only after their own greatness and wished to rule in Israel. To confirm his claim, he healed a lame man and a leper by the power of the Ineffable Name. For this, he was summoned before Queen Shalminon [or Helena], who found him guilty of acts of sorcery and beguilement.

But Yeshu restored a dead man to life, and the amazed Queen came to believe in him. He went next to Galilee, where he continued to work miracles and to attract crowds. The sages of Israel then saw that it was essential that one of their number, Yehuda Iskarioto, should learn the Ineffable Name, as Yeshu did, and rival him in signs and wonders. Yehuda and Yeshu came before the Queen. Yeshu flew in the air, but Yehuda flew higher and caused him to fall to the earth. Thereupon the Queen condemned Yeshu to death and delivered him up to the Sages of Israel. They took him to Tiberias [the city] and imprisoned him there. But he had taught his followers that whatever happened to him had been prepared for the Messiah, the Son of God, from the beginning of creation—that the prophets had foretold it all. The followers of Yeshu fought against the Sages of Israel, rescued him, and fled to Antioch.

From Antioch, Yeshu travelled to Egypt, where he learned spells. But Yehuda Iskarioto had [managed to] infiltrate the ranks of the disciples and to rob Yeshu of the Name. Hence, Yeshu went a second time to Jerusalem to learn the Name—and this Yehuda announced in advance to the Sages of Israel: When Yeshu should come to the Temple it was agreed that Yehuda would bow before him and thus the Sages would be able to distinguish between Yeshu and his disciples. [This was not easy, as all dressed in garments of one color.]

And so it happened that the Sages of Israel recognized him and arrested him. They took him out and hanged him on a cabbage stem. [This was done because Yeshu had adjured all trees by the Ineffable Name not to receive his body if he was hanged; but he had failed to adjure the cabbage stem.]

The body was taken down while it was still the eve of the Sabbath—in order not to violate the prohibition, "His body shall not remain there for the night"—and immediately buried. A gardener, Yehuda, removed the body from the tomb and cast it into a ditch and let the water flow over it.

The disciples, discovering that the body was not in the tomb, announced to the Queen that Yeshu had been restored to life. The Queen, believing the story, was tempted to put to death the Sages for having killed the Messiah. Indeed, all of the Jews mourned, wept and fasted, until Rabbi Tanchuma, with the help of God, found the body in a garden. The Sages of Israel removed it, tied it to the tail of a horse and paraded it in front of the Queen so that she could see the deception.

The disciples of Yeshu fled [for fear] and mingled among all nations. Among these followers were Twelve "apostles" who sorely distressed the Jews: one of these, Shimeon Kepha [Simon Peter] undertook to sepa-rate the disciples of Yeshu from the Jews and to give [the former]laws of their own. . . .

Greek and Latin Sources

JOSEPHUS

Flavius Josephus (Yoseph ben Mattathiah ha-Cohen) was born in 37 AD. His most famous works, written after the destruction of the Temple in 70, are *The Wars of the Jews* and *The Antiquities of the Jews,* both designed to explain the history of the Jewish nation and the reasons for the political unrest in Judea to literate and curious Romans. Given this purpose, Josephus might be expected to provide an account of the Jesus-movement that arose during the thirties and that was fast gaining ground by the seventies. Surprisingly, this is not the case. Josephus mentions Jesus only in passing, and this in a passage so heavily interpolated by later Christian scribes that the authenticity of the whole reference has frequently been doubted.

Scholars have often been troubled by the fact that—even granted the authenticity of a portion of the passage relating to Jesus—less space is accorded the "founder" of Christianity than to John the Baptist (*Ant.* 18.5.2), whom the Gospels depict as a decidedly inferior character. Further, the language used to describe John is very close to the language used to describe Jesus, leading some to theorize that the original version of the *Antiquities* carried no reference to Jesus at all.

All in all there is little reason to suppose that the whole of Josephus' account is spurious—though interpolations to the original text are probable. The *Antiquities* was written about the year 93, when the Christians constituted a large sect in Judea, Rome, and Asia Minor. A historian of Josephus' caliber could be expected to mention the founder of a Jewish sect that attracted many Greeks and Romans as well. In the passage that follows, I have italicized the passages which a majority of New Testament scholars regard as certainly or probably spurious.

> There was about this time [about the time of an uprising against Pilate] a wise man named Jesus *if it is permissible to call him a man.* He was in fact a doer of wonderful works, a teacher of such men as receive the truth gladly. He drew over to him both many Jews and not a few Gentiles. *He was the Messiah.*

> And when Pilate, at the suggestion of the principal men among us, had condemned him to the cross, those that loved him from the first continued to do so, *for he appeared to them alive again the third day as the divine Prophets had foretold these and ten thousand other wonderful things concerning him;* and the race of Christians, named for him, is not extinct even now.

Even if one accepts the non-italicized information as probably authentic, it is important to keep in mind that Josephus' comment offers absolutely nothing in the way of proof for the historical Jesus. Nothing he says adds to the Gospel account (already in written form by this date) or to the Christian missionary propaganda. The suggestion that "those who loved him at the first continued to do so," reflecting a background in the Christian-Gnostic controversies of the second century, was probably not written by Josephus. A more promising piece of evidence occurs elsewhere in the *Antiquities,* where Josephus tells how Annas, son of Annas the high priest, in the time between the death of the procurator Festus and his successor, Albinus,

> . . . lost no time in bringing before the Sanhedrin one named James, the brother of Jesus who was called the Messiah, and others he regarded as breakers of the law and condemned them to be stoned. [*Ant.* 20.9.1]

This passage too has suffered mutilation by Christian scribes—how much it is not possible to say. It is clear however from the context that James was executed as a seditionist, and may have been linked to the group known as *Sicarii* (dagger-men) who advocated open and militant opposition to the Roman forces (20.9.3). At least one of Jesus' disciples is remembered for his association with those rebels—Judas Iscariot.

To avoid implication in the troubles leading up to the destruction of the Temple, Christian legend recorded that the Jesus-sect had withdrawn to Pella, in Macedonia, prior to the Jewish rebellion. This legend is belied by the fact that Origen, an Alexandrian writer of the third century, quotes the *Antiquities* (an earlier version thereof) three times to the effect that the execution of James "the brother of the Jesus called Christ" was accomplished at the time of the siege of Jerusalem and led to the destruction of the Temple [*Comm. on Matthew,* 13.55; *Contra Celsum,* 1.47 and 2.13].

Finally, we turn to consider the Slavonic version of the *Wars of the Jews,* surviving in Russian and Rumanian but originally written in Greek. The passages relating to Jesus and John the Baptist are of particular interest, especially because they appear in part to preserve an earlier and more primitive version of the passages now contained in the *Antiquities.* The passages relating to John are presented here without comment. For those concerning Jesus, I have italicized those sentences that have no obvious claim to historical authenticity.

John the Forerunner

At that time a man was going about Judaea remarkably dressed: he wore animal hair on those parts of his body not covered by his own. His face was like a savage's. He called on the Jews to claim their freedom, crying:

"God sent me to show you the way of the Law, so that you can shake off any human yoke: no man shall rule you, but only the Most High who sent me." His message was eagerly welcomed, and he was followed by all Judaea and the district round Jerusalem. All he did was to baptize them in the Jordan and dismiss them with an earnest exhortation to abandon their evil ways: if they did so they would be given a king who would liberate them and master the unruly, while himself acknowledging no master. This promise was derided by some but believed by others.

The man was brought before Archelaus and an assemblage of lawyers, who asked who he was and where he had been. He replied: "I am a man called by the Spirit of God, and I live on stems, roots, and fruit." When he was threatened with torture if he did not stop behaving and talking like this, he retorted: "It would be more to the point if you stopped acting so disgracefully and submitted to the God you profess to worship."

Simon, a scribe of Essene origin, sprang up and exclaimed angrily: "We study Holy Writ every day; you have just come out of the forest like a wild animal; and do you dare put us right and mislead the people with your damnable nonsense?" Simon then rushed at him to tear him to pieces. But the man replied with a warning: "I will not reveal to you the secret that is in your midst, as you have refused to listen and so have brought immeasurable disaster upon your own heads." Then off he went to the other side of Jordan, where he resumed his work unmolested.

John, Philip and Antipas

During his reign Philip dreamt that an eagle pecked out both his eyes. He summoned his advisers, and when they had given a variety of interpretations in came unannounced the man mentioned above, who used to go round in animal hair and cleanse people in the River Jordan. He began: "Listen to God's message—the dream you had. The eagle, with its ferocious rapacity, represents your own cupidity—the sin that will cost you your two eyes; that is to say, your throne and your wife." Before sunset Philip was dead and his throne passed to Agrippa. His wife Herodias then married his brother Herod. This shocked and disgusted all who respected the Law, but they dared not take Herod to task. The man we referred to as a savage, and he alone, faced Herod and fiercely assailed him. "You have married your brother's wife in defiance of the Law, and just as he died a cruel death, so will divine vengeance bring your life to an end. The judgment of God is inexorable, and you are doomed to die miserably in exile. For *you* are not 'raising up seed unto your brother'; you are indulging in your own lust and committing adultery, considering that he has left four children." This attack infuriated Herod, who ordered the man to be flogged and kicked out. But he constantly waylaid the tetrach and reiterated his accusations, till Herod lost control altogether and ordered him to be killed.

He was a strange creature, not like a man at all. He lived like a disembodied spirit. He never touched bread; even at the Passover Feast he would not eat the unleavened bread or pronounce the words "In thankfulness to God, who delivered the nation from slavery, shall you eat this; it was given for the flight, because the journey was made in haste." Wine and other strong drink he would not allow to be brought anywhere near him, and animal food he absolutely refused—fruit was all that he needed. The whole object of his life was to show evil in its true colours.

The Ministry and Crucifixion of Jesus

It was at that time that a man appeared —*if "man" is the right word— who had all the attributes of a man but seemed to be something greater. His actions, certainly, were superhuman, for he worked such wonderful and amazing miracles that I for one cannot regard him as a man; yet in view of his likeness to ourselves I cannot regard him as an angel either.* Everything that some hidden power enabled him to do he did by an authoritative word. Some people said that their first Lawgiver had risen from the dead and had effected many marvelous cures; other thought he was a messenger from heaven. However, in many ways he broke the Law—for instance, he did not observe the Sabbath in the traditional manner. At the same time his conduct was above reproach. He did not need to use his hands: a word sufficed to fulfil his every purpose.

Many of the common people flocked after him and followed his teaching. There was a wave of excited expectation that he would enable the Jewish tribes to throw off the Roman yoke. As a rule he was to be found opposite the City on the Mount of Olives, where also he healed the sick. He gathered round him 150 assistants and masses of followers. When they saw his ability to do whatever he wished by a word, they told him that they wanted him to enter the City, destroy the Roman troops, and make himself king; but he took no notice.

When the suggestion came to the ears of the Jewish authorities, they met under the chairmanship of the high priest and exclaimed: "We are utterly incapable of resisting the Romans; but as the blow is about to fall we'd better go and tell Pilate what we've heard, and steer clear of trouble, in case he gets to know from someone else and confiscates our property, puts us to death, and turns our children adrift." So they went and told Pilate, who sent troops and butchered many of the common people. He then had the Miracle-worker brought before him, held an inquiry, and expresssed the opinion that he was a benefactor, not a criminal or agitator or a would-be king. Then he let them go, as he had cured Pilate's wife when she was at the point of death.

Returning to his usual haunts he resumed his normal work. When the crowds grew bigger than ever, he earned by his actions an incomparable reputation. The exponents of the Law were mad with jealousy, and gave Pilate 30 talents to have him executed. Accepting this bribe, he gave them permission to carry out their wishes themselves. So they seized him and crucified him in defiance of all Jewish tradition.

In the time of Cuspius Fadus and Tiberius Alexander many of the Miracle-worker's followers came forward and declared to the adherents of their master that, although he had died, he was now alive and would free them from their slavery. Many of the common people listened to their preaching and accepted their call—not because they were men of mark, for they were working men, some only shoemakers, others cobblers, others labourers. But they worked marvellous "signs"; in fact nothing was beyond their power.

Seeing the unsettlement of the people, these excellent procurators decided after consulting the scribes to arrest the men and put them to death, for fear that the movement, though of no consequence at the moment, might end in a major upheaval. But in face of the "signs" they hesitated and dared not take any action, convinced that no medical treatment could account for such marvellous cures, and surmising that if these were not the work of God himself they would soon be shown up.

So they gave the men complete freedom of action. Later, however, they were persuaded by the scribes to send them to Rome or Antioch to be tried, banishing others to distant countries.

The Rending of the Veil and the Resurrection

In the days of our pious fathers this curtain was intact, but in our own generation it was a sorry sight, for it has been suddenly rent from top to bottom at the time when by bribery they had secured the execution of the benefactor of men—the one who by his actions proved that he was no mere man. Many other awe-inspiring "signs" happened at the same time. It is also stated that after his execution and entombment he disappeared entirely. Some people actually assert that he had risen; others retort that his friends stole him away. I for one cannot decide where the truth lies. A dead man cannot rise by his own power; but he might rise if aided by the prayer of another righteous man. Again, if an angel or other heavenly being, or God Himself, takes human form to fulfill his purpose, and after living among men dies and is buried, he can rise again at will. Moreover it is stated that he could not have been stolen away, as guards were posted round his tomb, 30 Romans and 1,000 Jews.

TACITUS, *ANNALS OF IMPERIAL ROME*

Thus far we have considered Jewish (Hebrew) and Greek-Jewish sources. The Latin, non-Jewish sources are not extensive, and none is contemporary with the teaching career of Jesus himself. The earliest of these comes in the annals of the Roman historian Tacitus (written about 115 AD), in the course of his discussion of the burning of Rome in the time of Nero (64 AD). According to Tacitus, Nero wished to avert suspicion that he himself had set the fire and found ready scapegoats in the new Christian sect. Tacitus' opinion of the sect is typical of that of the Roman intellectual class of the second century. In evaluating his testimony, however, one should be aware that it does not add substantially to the stock of knowledge about Jesus propagated in Rome by Christian missionaries. That Tacitus gleaned his facts from other sources is doubtful.

But neither human resources, nor imperial munificence, nor appeasement of the gods, eliminated sinister suspicions that the fire had been instigated. To suppress this rumour, Nero fabricated scapegoats—and punished with every refinement the notoriously depraved Christians (as they were popularly called). Their originator, Christ, had been executed in Tiberius' reign by the governor of Judaea, Pontius Pilatus. But in spite of this temporary setback the deadly superstition had broken out afresh, not only in Judaea (where the mischief had started) but even in Rome. All degraded and shameful practices collect and flourish in the capital.

First, Nero had self-acknowledged Christians arrested. Then, on their information, large numbers of others were condemned—not so much for incendiarism as for their anti-social tendencies. Their deaths were made farcical. Dressed in wild animals' skins, they were torn to pieces by dogs, or crucified, or made into torches to be ignited after dark as substitutes for daylight. Nero provided his Gardens for the spectacle, and exhibited displays in the Circus, at which he mingled with the crowd—or stood in a chariot, dressed as a charioteer. Despite their guilt as Christians, and the ruthless punishment it deserved, the victims were pitied. For it was felt that they were being sacrificed to one man's brutality rather than to the national interest. [*Annals* 15.43]

SUETONIUS, *THE TWELVE CAESARS*

The evidence of the historian Suetonius (65-135) is no earlier than that supplied by Tacitus, and far more ambiguous. While dealing in his *Twelve Caesars* with the emperor Claudius, he writes: *"Judaeos impulsore Chresto assidue tumultuantes Roma expulit,"* that is, "He banished the Jews from Rome, since they had made a commotion because of Chrestus."

This "expulsion" may be the one referred to in the Acts of the

Apostles (18:2), where we learn that Aquila of Pontus and his wife Priscilla came from Italy during the time of Paul's missionary work "because of Claudius' decree that all Jews should leave Rome." According to Orosius, the expulsion took place in Claudius' ninth year as Caesar (49 AD). It is not entirely clear whether the reference to Chrestus is to a rebel actively inciting the Jews to violence—if so it can hardly be a reference to Jesus—or to a movement taking its impetus from someone known as Chrestus (Christos).

Alternatively, Suetonius may simply be referring, in honest ignorance, to a messianic movement of no certain vintage: the Greek word *Christos*, (= Messiah) badly transliterated as *Christos* permits no certain identification of an historical individual, and most of those who find Suetonius' reference an allusion to Jesus make the identification on the basis of an unhistorical bias. In short, there is little likelihood, in the context of the passage, that the Chrestus mentioned by Suetonius is Jesus of Nazareth.

Elsewhere in the *Twelve Caesars*, namely in his discussions of Nero's reign, Suetonius mentions the Christians as a "new and mischievous" sect, but appears to know nothing of their origin in Judaea or of the founder.

Nero introduced his own new style of architecture in the city: building out porches from the fronts of apartments and private houses to serve as fire-fighting platforms, and subsidizing the work himself. He also considered a scheme for extending the city wall as far as Ostia, and cutting a canal which would allow ships to sail straight up to Rome.

During his reign a great many public abuses were suppressed by the imposition of heavy penalties, and among the equally numerous novel enactments were sumptuary laws limiting private expenditure; the substitution of a simple grain distribution for public banquets; and a decree restricting the food sold in wine-shops to green vegetables and dried beans—whereas before all kinds of snacks had been displayed. Punishments were also inflicted on the Christians, a sect professing a new and mischievous religious belief; and Nero ended the licence which the charioteers had so long enjoyed that they claimed it as a right: to wander down the streets, swindling and robbing the populace. [Nero, 16]

Literary Forgeries

Beginning in the second century, pseudonymous[7] letters began to appear, purporting to contain documentary evidence for the life, crucifixion, and resurrection of Jesus. Hence we possess a large number of literary forgeries ascribed to the principals in the New Testament story: Pilate, Herod, Joseph of Arimathea, and even Tiberius. Christianity was not unique in the production of such forgeries. It was long the custom in the Hellenistic world to garner support for belief in a movement by inventing authoritative endorsements where none could be found to exist. Jewish apocalyptic writings, for example, normally bear the name of one of the Old Testament worthies—Daniel, Enoch, Ezra—who lived centuries before the books credited to them were written. In the New Testament itself, only a minority of the letters attributed to Paul were actually written by him, the greater number being devised to settle later doctrinal disputes on the basis of his authority. Indeed, many New Testament scholars consider it improbable that any New Testament writing, with the exception of the genuine letters of Paul, bears the name of its true author.

The association of certain writings with prestigious writers, especially "apostolic" authors such as John, Matthew, Peter, and James is a development best understood in terms of the history of the New Testament canon, where such association was necessary to guarantee the survival of otherwise anonymous or (in many cases) composite creations. In general, however, modern scholars consider the traditional view of the New Testament writings—accounts produced by Jesus' followers and their disciples—completely untenable.

The following selections represent a further development in early Christian propaganda; in essence, they are pious forgeries designed to convert wavering Gentiles to the faith or to demonstrate to the merely curious that Jesus had secured the belief of his persecutors. By this literary contrivance, a church faced with persecution hoped to persuade Roman officialdom of its error: Jesus (so these documents maintain) had been recognized as a God and savior even by those responsible for his execution. A comparable motif is to be found in the Gospels, in the pericope known as the "Centurion's confession" (Mark

15:39), as well as in John's flattering view of Pilate (John 19:4-12). Out of this raw material, the following "documents" were fashioned.

THE LETTERS OF PILATE AND HEROD

These letters exist in Greek and Syriac manuscripts of the sixth century, though they go back to a much earlier Greek original. The so-called *Acts of Pilate,* to which the letters are appended, is known to a second-century writer, Justin Martyr, himself a Syriac presbyter. The favorable view of Pilate is characteristic of the Eastern Church; in the Coptic church, he is revered as a martyr. The conflict of church and synagogue is prominent in both epistles.

The Letter of Pilate to Herod

It was no good thing which I did at your persuasion when I crucified Jesus. I ascertained from the centurion and the soliders that he rose again, and I sent to Galilee and learned that he was preaching there to above five hundred believers.

My wife Procla took Longinus, the believing centurion, and ten soldiers (who had kept the sepulchre), and went forth and found him "sitting in a tilled field" teaching a multitude. He saw them, addressed them, and spoke of his victory over death and hell. Procla and the rest returned and told me. I was in great distress, and put on a mourning garment and went with her and fifty soldiers to Galilee. We found Jesus: and as we approached him there was a sound in heaven and thunder, and the earth trembled and gave forth a sweet odour. We fell on our faces and the Lord came and raised us up, and I saw on him the scars of the passion, and he laid his hands on my shoulders, saying: All generations and families shall call thee blessed . . . because in thy days the Son of Man died and rose again.

The Letter of Herod to Pilate

It is in no small sorrow—according to the divine Scriptures—that I write to you.

My dear daughter Herodias was playing upon the ice and fell in up to her neck. And her mother caught at her head to save her, and it was cut off, and the water swept her body away. My wife is sitting with the head on her knees, weeping, and all the house is full of sorrow.

I am in great distress of mind at the death of Jesus, and reflecting on my sins in killing John the Baptist and massacring the Innocents. Since, then, you are able to see the man Jesus again, strive for me and intercede for me: for to you Gentiles the kingdom is given, according to the prophets and Christ.

Lesbonax my son is in the last stages of a decline. I am afflicted with dropsy, and worms are coming out of my mouth. My wife's left eye is blinded through weeping. Righteous are the judgments of God, because we mocked at the eye of the righteous. Vengeance will come on the Jews and the priests, and the Gentiles will inherit the kingdom, and the children of light be cast out.

And Pilate, since we are of one age, bury my family honorably: it is better for us to be buried by you than by the priests, who are doomed to speedy destruction. Farewell. I have sent you my wife's earrings and my own signet ring. I am already beginning to receive judgment in this world, but I fear the judgment hereafter much more. This is temporary, that is everlasting.

THE LETTER OF TIBERIUS

The following, dating from an eighth-century version of an earlier legend, paints Pilate in a more villainous light (typical of Western churches) and offers up the ludicrous suggestion that a strangely "Christian" Tiberius had sent two soldiers led by a certain messenger named Raab, to bring Pilate to justice in Rome.

Letter of Tiberius to Pilate

[This was delivered to Pilate by means of the messenger Raab (cf. Rachaab in Recension B) who was sent with 2,000 soldiers to bring him to Rome.]

Since you have given a violent and iniquitous sentence of death against Jesus of Nazareth, showing no pity, and having received gifts to condemn him, and with your tongue have expressed sympathy [a reference to the Anaphora], but in your heart have delivered him up, you shall be brought home a prisoner to answer for yourself.

I have been exceedingly distressed at the reports that have reached me: a woman, a disciple of Jesus, has been here, called Mary Magdalene, out of whom he is said to have cast seven devils, and has told of all his wonderful cures. How could you permit him to be crucified? If you did not receive him as a God, you might at least have honoured him as a physician. Your own deceitful writing to me has condemned you.

As you unjustly sentenced him, I shall justly sentence you, and your accomplices as well.

ACTS OF PETER AND PAUL

This apocryphal work in Greek dating from the third century includes the following "Letter of Pilate to the Emperor Claudius." The author of the letter has overlooked the fact that Pilate was governor of Judaea only until 36 AD; Claudius did not become emperor until 41. Central to the purpose of the letter is the writer's insistence that Jesus' body had not been stolen from the tomb as the Jews alleged.

Letter of Pilate to Claudius

Pontius Pilate to his emperor Claudius, greeting. There happened recently something which I myself brought to light. The Jews through envy have punished themselves and their posterity with a fearful judgment. For their fathers had received the promise that God would send them from heaven his holy one, who would rightly be called their king and whom God has promised to send to earth by a virgin. But when he came to Judaea when I was governor, and they saw that he restored sight to the blind, cleansed lepers, healed paralytics, expelled evil spirits from men, and even raised the dead, and commanded the winds, and walked dry-shod upon the waves of the sea, and did many other miracles, and all the people of the Jews acknowledged him to be the Son of God, the chief priests were moved by envy against him, and they seized him and delivered him to me, and bringing forward lie after lie they accused him of being a sorcerer and transgressing their law. And I

believed this was so, and ordered him to be scourged, and handed him
-over to their will. And they crucified him, and set guards at his tomb.
But he rose again on the third day, while my soldiers kept watch. But
the Jews were so carried away with their wickedness that they gave
money to my soldiers, saying, "Say that his disciples stole his body." But
although they took the money, they were unable to keep silent about
what had happened. For they testified that he had arisen, and that they
had seen it, and that they had received money from the Jews. I have
reported this lest anyone should lie about the matter and you should
think that the lies of the Jews should be believed.

THE LETTER OF LENTULUS

The letter ascribed to Publius Lentulus, who calls himself "Governor
of Jerusalem," is a pious forgery—roughly the literary equivalent of
such acheiropoietic images as Veronica's veil and the Shroud of Turin.
Apart from the fact that there was no "governor" of Jerusalem in
Jesus' day, this letter does not seem to have been widely known in the
West prior to the fourteenth century. By this time, a variety of reports
had circulated—notably those of Nicephorus Callistus (in a tenth century chronicle) and John Damascene (eighth century)—which included
elaborate physical descriptions of Jesus. In all likelihood, these letters
describe iconographic likenesses well known in the Near East by the
beginning of the Middle Ages.

A certain Lentulus, a Roman, being an official for the Romans in the
province of Judaea in the time of Tiberius Caesar, upon seeing Christ,
and noting his wonderful works, his preaching, his endless miracles,
and other amazing things about him, wrote thus to the Roman senate:
"There hath appeared in these times, and still is, a man of great power
named Jesus Christ, who is called by the Gentiles (peoples) the prophet
of truth, whom his disciples call the Son of God: raising the dead and
healing diseases, a man in stature middling tall, and comely, having a
reverend countenance, which they that look upon may love and fear;
having hair the hue of an unripe hazel-nut and smooth almost down to
his ears, but from the ears in curling locks somewhat darker and more
shining, waving over (from) his shoulders; having a parting in the mid-

dle of the head according to the fashion of the Nazareans; a brow smooth and very calm, with a face without a wrinkle or any blemish, which a moderate colour (red) makes beautiful; with the nose and mouth no fault at all can be found; having a full beard of the colour of his hair, not long, but a little forked at the chin; having an expression simple and mature, the eyes grey, glancing(?) (various) and clear; in rebuke terrible, in admonition kind and lovable, cheerful yet keeping gravity; sometimes he hath wept, but never laughed; in stature of body tall and straight, with hands and arms fair to look upon; in talk grave, reserved and modest [so that he was rightly called by the prophet] fairer than the children of men."

THE LETTERS OF JESUS AND ABGARUS

This correspondence is provided by the fourth-century writer, Eusebius of Caesarea in his *Ecclesiastical History* (1.13). Eusebius claims, improbably, that he extracted it from the archives of Edessa relating to Abgarus—king of Edessa (4 BC-50 AD). A later tradition maintained that the letter of Christ was written (in Syriac) on parchment and survived for many years. Among the additions to the legend is the story that Jesus sent his portrait, imprinted on a linen cloth, along with the letter to the king. The best estimate is that the letter was written some time after the conversion of Abgar IV (179-214), but it was long regarded as authentic by Syriac Christians.

Letter of Abgarus

[A copy of a letter written by Abgarus the toparch to Jesus, and sent to him by means of Ananias the runner, to Jerusalem.]

Abgarus Uchama the toparch to Jesus the good Saviour that hath appeared in the parts (place) of Jerusalem, greeting. I have heard concerning thee and thy cures, that they are done of thee without drugs or herbs: for, as the report goes, thou makest blind men to see again, lame to walk, and cleanest lepers, and castest out unclean spirits and devils, and those that are afflicted with long sickness thou healest, and raisest the dead. And having heard all this of thee, I had determined one of two things, either that thou art God come down from heaven, and so doest these things, or art a Son of God that doest these things. Therefore now have I written and entreated thee to trouble thyself *to come* to me and heal the affliction which I have. For indeed I have heard that the Jews even murmur against thee and wish to do thee hurt. And I have a very little city but (and) comely (reverend), which is sufficient to us both.

Letter of Jesus

[The answer, written by Jesus, sent by Ananias the runner to Abgarus the toparch.]

Blessed are thou that hast believed in me, not having seen me. For it is written concerning me that they that have seen me shall not believe in me, and that they that have not seen me shall believe and live. But concerning that which thou hast written to me, to come unto thee; it must needs be that I fulfill all things for the which I was sent here, and after fulfilling them should then be taken up unto him that sent me. And when I am taken up, I will send thee one of my disciples, to heal thine affliction and give life to thee and them that are with thee.

Sayings Attributed to Jesus

The Gospels remain the most extensive sources of the sayings of Jesus. Scholars now generally recognize that few, if any, of these sayings can be considered words that Jesus spoke during his lifetime. At best, they represent a reminiscence—hence an interpretation—of his sayings, altered to suit the time and the circumstances of their composition and the audience to which they were directed. The changing situation of the early Jesus-believers entailed that some words would be remembered (for example, those concerning persecution); some radically altered (for example, those concerning the Last Days); and others selectively erased or softened (presumably, threats against the Temple: see Mark 15:29).

Just as the prosaic and ordinary was destined to be forgotten, moral teachings, parables, and "prophecies" relevant to the life of the community were given an enduring lease of life in the social memory of the early Christian teachers. So too were the sayings that have the least to do with the historical Jesus: namely, those that portray Jesus as calling himself the Son of God, and announcing his divine sonship to the world. Careful readers of the Synoptic Gospels will appreciate at once the difference in style between the Jesus of Mark (for example 6:4) and the divine-man of the Fourth Gospel (John 10:30).

"Sayings" of Jesus—which might better be termed traditions *about* the sayings of Jesus—are not confined to the Gospels canonized in the New Testament. There exist scores of sayings *(logia)* for which there are no parallels, or only distant ones, in the Gospels. Collectively, these go by the misleading name *agrapha*—unrecorded words. As this title prejudices their analysis (the Gospels do not present a verbatim record of Jesus' words), it is best to designate them "extracanonical" sayings or sayings-traditions. The significance of these sayings, it should be emphasized, is *not* that they present a more reliable picture of Jesus than the one given in the Synoptic Gospels. Rather, they put it beyond doubt that the church was capable of generating sayings to suit new situations, and did not hesitate to invent new "words" of the Lord in furthering their missionary work. The questions of proselytes and the accusations of enemies of the sect were the most prominent but by no means the only situations addressed by these sayings. Since it is not possible to offer the full range of *agrapha* here, what follows is a sample of *logia* extracted from the letters of Paul and other early Christian writers.

PAUL'S LETTERS

The earliest of all Christian writings come from Paul, who was not himself a follower of Jesus during the latter's lifetime. Moreover, as we have noted, Paul was not especially interested in the "historicity" of Jesus, preferring instead the divine-man christology that he had learned from his dabbling in Greek philosophy. Hence, it is to be expected that in Paul's *genuine* letters we find almost no reference to the life and teaching of Jesus, and very few sayings. This comparative indifference to history in the earliest phase of the development of the new sect stands in conflict with the fact that sayings *attributed* to Jesus multiply over the course of time—a difficulty that is not resolved by the familiar argument that Paul, as not being an eyewitness to the ministry of Jesus, would not have known many of his sayings. The very fact that the earliest Christian literature *lacks* such sayings serves to indicate that in Paul's day the *teaching* of Jesus was not considered as important as *beliefs* about him, beliefs that had the effect of altering and eroding historical data. What survives can be given as follows:

> The new tradition which I handed on to you came to me from the Lord himself: that the Lord Jesus, on the night of his arrest, took bread, and after giving thanks to God, broke it and said, "This is my body, which is for you; do this as a memorial of me." In the same way, he took the cup after supper and said, "This cup is the new covenant sealed in my blood. Whenever you drink it, do this as a memorial of me." [1 Cor. 11:23-25]

> "Let not a woman separate from her husband." [1 Cor 7:10]

> "Let those that preach the gospel live by the gospel." [1 Cor. 9:14]

Famous but of dubious vintage is a saying attributed by Paul to Jesus in the Acts of the Apostles: "It is better to give than to receive" [Acts 20:35].

SAYINGS OCCURRING IN EARLY CHRISTIAN LITERATURE

Scattered throughout the works of early Christian writers from Justin Martyr (fl. 160 AD) onward are a number of sayings attributed to Jesus that have no parallels in the canonical gospels. Some, for example those preserved by the theologian Origen, suggest that Jesus was preoccupied with the signs and material blessings surrounding the millennium; others, especially those related by Clement of Alexandria, imply that Jesus was thoroughly antimaterialistic and was only concerned to teach the truth about his relation to God, as he does for example in the Fourth Gospel and the gnostic *Gospel of Thomas* (pp. 74–86). The process of selection and preservation of these *logia* is a reflection of the theological concerns of individual writers working in particular historical settings—or put another way, Jesus is given to say those things individual writers find it convenient for him to say. What follows is a sampling of the more important of these sayings:

"I shall judge you where I find you." [Justin, *Dial. with Trypho*, 47]

"Ask for what is important and the small things will come of their own; ask for heavenly things, and the earthly shall be added to them." [Origen, *On Prayer*, 2]

"Be competent money-changers." [Clement of Alexandria, *Miscellanies*, 1.28.177]

"Let not the lambs fear the wolves, after they are dead. Do not fear those who persecute you [but] can do nothing to harm you—Rather fear him who, after you are dead, has power over body and soul to cast them into hell fire." [*Second Epistle of Clement*, 5.2-4]

"Be saved: Save your soul." [Clement of Alexandria, *Excerpt from Theodorus*, 2]

"No man that is not tempted shall obtain the kingdom of God." [Tertullian, *On Baptism*, 20]

"A man not tempted is not approved." [Didascalia, 2.8]

"He that is near me is near the fire; but he that is far from me is far from the kingdom." [Origen, *On Jeremiah*, 3.3]

"You must keep the secrets for me and those of my house." [Clementine Homilies 19.20]

"Many shall come in my name, clad in sheep skins, who are inwardly

ravenous wolves: There will be divisions and heresies." [Justin, *Dial.
with Trypho* 35]

"If you do not make the left hand as the right and the right as the left
and the things above as those that are below and the things that are
before as those behind, you shall not know the kingdom of God."
[*Martyrdom of Peter* 17]

"The day shall come when vines will grow ten thousand branches each,
and each branch ten thousand shoots, each shoot ten thousand clusters
and every cluster ten thousand grapes—and every grape when it is pressed
shall yield twenty-five portions of wine. And when any of the saints
takes hold of a cluster, another will cry out, 'I am the better cluster: take
me and do homage to God.'" [Irenaeus, *Against Heresies* 5.33.3; cf.
Apocalypse of Baruch 29.5]

[Judas asks Jesus who shall see the kingdom] "These things shall they
see who are worthy." [Hippolytus, *Daniel* 4.60]

"I came to destroy the sacrifices; if you do not cease from sacrificing, the
wrath of God will not cease from you." [Epiphanius, *Against Heresies*
30]

"If anyone in Israel will repent to believe in God through my name, his
sins will be forgiven him. And after twelve years, go out into the world,
lest anyone say, We did not hear." [Clement of Alexandria, *Miscellanies*
6.5.39]

"Those who are with me have not understood me." [*Actus Vercellenses*,
10]

"He who today stands far off, tomorrow will be near to you." [*Oxyrhyn-
chus papyrus* 1224, c. 300]

[He saw a man doing work on the Sabbath and said to him] "Man, if
you are aware of what you are doing, blessed are you! But if you do not
know, then you are to be condemned as a transgressor of the law."
[Codex D version of Luke 6:4]

"The years of Satan's power have come to an end; but terrible things await those on whose account, as sinners, I was delivered up to death so that they could follow the truth and sin no more." [Freer logion of Mark 16:14, fifth century, labeled "W"]

"My mother, the Holy Spirit, took me by the hair and carried me away to Mount Tabor." [Origen, *Commentary on John*, 2:12.87; cf. John 1:3]

"He that marvels shall reign and he that reigns shall rest." [Clement of Alexandria, *Miscellanies*, 2.9.45]

"Never be joyful, save when you observe your brother with love." [Jerome, *Commentary on Ephesians* 3]

As a special case it is necessary to mention the frequently quoted saying found as an inscription on the south main portal of the mosque in Fathpur-Sikri, India. The mosque dates from 1601, but the saying occurs in Islamic literature from the eighth century onward: "Jesus, on whom be peace, said: 'The world is a bridge: go over it, but do not come to rest upon it.'"

Gnostic Literature

The discovery of a cache of thirteen papyri in Nag Hammadi (Upper Egypt) in 1945–1946 caused considerable excitement among scholars. The forty-nine individual writings are dated between the third and fifth centuries and written in Coptic, having been translated from Greek. The Nag Hammadi treatises, now available in English translation,[8] were produced and preserved by Gnostic Christians and constitute our most direct evidence for this fascinating variety of early Christianity. The name *gnostic* derives from the Greek word *gnōsis*, or knowledge, and was used descriptively by the church fathers, especially Irenaeus, to mean a movement centering on the following tenets: (1) creation is the work of an inferior god and marks a decline in the perfection of the divine fullness (*pleroma*). (2) Mankind (or a select few), though under the power of the lesser god and his minions (Archons), can be saved by a secret knowledge. (3) This secret is imparted by a revealer-savior figure, whose message contains instructions of how the elect can bypass the powers of darkness and return to the primordial light.

Since gnosticism thrived on complexity, one must speak of individual "systems" or "schools" of gnosticism, each with its own characteristic doctrines. In Christian gnosticism generally the Old Testament god was identified with the inferior god (akin to the demiurge of Plato), and Jesus—especially in his post-resurrection appearances—with the savior-revealer. Not surprisingly, the Gospel of John, itself influenced by Gnostic ideas, and the letters of Paul were especially revered by Gnostic Christians. Certain Christian fathers, notably Clement of Alexandria (150-215), openly embraced Gnostic tenets, and Christianity as a whole assimilated more of the heresy than the early writers imagined.

THE GOSPEL OF THOMAS

This gospel, now preserved in the Coptic Museum in Cairo, is perhaps the most famous and the most unusual of the treatises found in Nag Hammadi. In form, it is not a gospel at all, but rather a series of sayings and (often perplexing) discourses. Since an original Greek version may date from the early second century, it has been suggested that the *Gospel* may preserve sayings in a form *earlier* than those found in the canonical Gospels. No judicious scholar can seriously entertain such a claim, since we lack any solid criterion for determining what might be "older" than a canonical saying. From an historical standpoint, the value of *The Gospel of Thomas* is not that it offers us a reliable picture of Jesus of Nazareth; rather, it is eloquent testimony to how quickly the historical figure and his teaching were transformed into a literary genre ("revealer-discourse") and brought into the service of a particular movement. In reading *The Gospel of Thomas* impartially, we are better equipped to see how a movement that opposed gnosticism, later to be designated "orthodoxy" or "catholicism," generated sayings to suit *its* purposes.

The Gospel of Thomas

II 32, 10-51, 28

These are the secret sayings which the living Jesus spoke and which Didymos Judas Thomas wrote down.

(1) And he said, "Whoever finds the interpretation of these sayings will not experience death."

(2) Jesus said, "Let him who seeks continue seeking until he finds. When he finds, he will become troubled. When he becomes troubled, he will be astonished, and he will rule over the All."

(3) Jesus said, "If those who lead you say to you, 'See, the Kingdom is in the sky,' then the birds of the sky will precede you. If they say to you, 'It is in the sea,' then the fish will precede you. Rather, the Kingdom is inside of you, and it is outside of you. When you come to know yourselves, then you will become known, and you will realize that it is you who are the sons of the living Father. But if you will not know yourselves, you dwell in poverty and it is you who are that poverty."

(4) Jesus said, "The man old in days will not hesitate to ask a small child seven days old about the place of life, and he will live. For many who are first will become last, and they will become one and the same."

(5) Jesus said, "Recognize what is in your sight, and that which is hidden from you will become plain to you. For there is nothing hidden which will not become manifest."

(6) His disciples questioned Him and said to Him, "Do You want us to fast? How shall we pray? Shall we give alms? What diet shall we observe?"

Jesus said, "Do not tell lies, and do not do what you hate, for all things are plain in the sight of Heaven. For nothing hidden will not become manifest, and nothing covered will remain without being uncovered."

(7) Jesus said, "Blessed is the lion which becomes man when consumed by man; and cursed is the man whom the lion consumes, and the lion becomes man."

(8) And He said, "The man is like a wise fisherman who cast his net into the sea and drew it up from the sea full of small fish. Among them the wise fisherman found a fine large fish. He threw all the small fish back into the sea

and chose the large fish without difficulty. Whoever has ears to hear, let him hear."

(9) Jesus said, "Now the sower went out, took a handful (of seeds), and scattered them. Some fell on the road; the birds came and gathered them up. Others fell on rock, did not take root in the soil, and did not produce ears. And others fell on thorns; they choked the seed(s) and worms ate them. And others fell on the good soil and produced good fruit; it bore sixty per measure and a hundred and twenty per measure."

(10) Jesus said, "I have cast fire upon the world, and see, I am guarding it until it blazes."

(11) Jesus said, "This heaven will pass away, and the one above it will pass away. The dead are not alive, and the living will not die. In the days when you consumed what is dead, you made it what is alive. When you come to dwell in the light, what will you do? On the day when you were one you became two. But when you become two, what will you do?"

(12) The disciples said to Jesus, "We know that You will depart from us. Who is to be our leader?"

Jesus said to them, "Wherever you are, you are to go to James the righteous, for whose sake heaven and earth came into being."

(13) Jesus said to His disciples, "Compare me to someone and tell me whom I am like."

Simon Peter said to Him, "You are like a righteous angel."

Matthew said to Him, "You are like a wise philosopher."

Thomas said to Him, "Master, my mouth is wholly incapable of saying whom You are like."

Jesus said, "I am not your master. Because you have drunk, you have become intoxicated from the bubbling spring which I have measured out."

And he took him and withdrew and told him three things. When Thomas returned to his companions, they asked him, "What did Jesus say to you?"

Thomas said to them, "If I tell you one of the things which he told me, you will pick up stones and throw them at me; a fire will come out of the stones and burn you up."

(14) Jesus said to them, "If you fast, you will give rise to sin for yourselves; and if you pray, you will be condemned; and if you give alms, you will do harm to your spirits. When you go into any land and walk about in the districts, if they receive you, eat what they will set before you, and heal the sick among them. For what goes into your mouth will not defile you, but that which issues from your mouth—it is that which will defile you."

(15) Jesus said, "When you see one who was not born of woman, prostrate

yourselves on your faces and worship him. That one is your Father."

(16) Jesus said, "Men think, perhaps, that it is peace which I have come to cast upon the world. They do not know that it is dissension which I have come to cast upon the earth: fire, sword, and war. For there will be five in a house: three will be against two, and two against three, the father against the son, and the son against the father. And they will stand solitary."

(17) Jesus said, "I shall give you what no eye has seen and what no ear has heard and what no hand has touched and what has never occurred to the human mind."

(18) The disciples said to Jesus, "Tell us how our end will be."

Jesus said, "Have you discovered, then, the beginning, that you look for the end? For where the beginning is, there will the end be. Blessed is he who will take his place in the beginning; he will know the end and will not experience death."

(19) Jesus said, "Blessed is he who came into being before he came into being. If you become My disciples and listen to My words, these stones will minister to you. For there are five trees for you in Paradise which remain undisturbed summer and winter and whose leaves do not fall. Whoever becomes acquainted with them will not experience death."

(20) The disciples said to Jesus, "Tell us what the Kingdom of Heaven is like."

He said to them, "It is like a mustard seed, the smallest of all seeds. But when it falls on tilled soil, it produces a great plant and becomes a shelter for birds of the sky."

(21) Mary said to Jesus, "Whom are Your disciples like?"

He said, "They are like children who have settled in a field which is not theirs. When the owners of the field come, they will say, 'Let us have back our field.' They (will) undress in their presence in order to let them have back their field and give it back to them. Therefore I say to you, if the owner of a house knows that the thief is coming, he will begin his vigil before he comes and will not let him dig through into his house of his domain to carry away his goods. You, then, be on your guard against the world. Arm yourselves with great strength lest the robbers find a way to come to you, for the difficulty which you expect will (surely) materialize. Let there be among you a man of understanding. When the grain ripened, he came quickly with his sickle in his hand and reaped it. Whoever has ears to hear, let him hear."

(22) Jesus saw infants being suckled. He said to His disciples, "These infants being suckled are like those who enter the Kingdom."

They said to Him, "Shall we then, as children, enter the Kingdom?"

Jesus said to them, "When you make the two one, and when you make the inside like the outside and the outside like the inside, and the above like the below, and when you make the male and the female one and the same, so that the male not be male nor the female female; and when you fashion eyes in place of an eye, and a hand in place of a hand, and a foot in place of a foot, and a likeness in place of a likeness, then you will enter l[the Kingdomį."

(23) Jesus said, "I shall choose you, one out of a thousand, and two out of ten thousand, and they shall stand as a single one."

(24) His disciples said to Him, "Show us the place where You are, since it is necessary for us to seek it."

He said to them, "Whoever has ears, let him hear. There is light within a man of light, and he [or: it] lights up the whole world. If he [or: it] does not shine, he [or: it] is darkness."

(25) Jesus said, "Love your brother like your soul, guard him like the pupil of your eye."

(26) Jesus said, "You see the mote in your brother's eye, but you do not see the beam in your own eye. When you cast the beam out of your own eye, then you will see clearly to cast the mote from your brother's eye."

(27) [Jesus said,] "If you do not fast as regards the world, you will not find the kingdom. If you do not observe the Sabbath as a Sabbath, you will not see the Father."

(28) Jesus said, "I took My place in the midst of the world, and I appeared to them in flesh. I found all of them intoxicated; I found none of them thirsty. And My soul became afflicted for the sons of men, because they are blind in their hearts and do not have sight; for empty they came into the world, and empty too they seek to leave the world. But for the moment they are intoxicated. When they shake off their wine, then they will repent."

(29) Jesus said, "If the flesh came into being because of spirit, it is a wonder. But if spirit came into being because of the body, it is a wonder of wonders. Indeed, I am amazed at how this great wealth has made its home in this poverty."

(30) Jesus said, "Where there are three gods, they are gods. Where there are two or one, I am with him."

(31) Jesus said, "No prophet is accepted in his own village; no physician heals those who know him."

(32) Jesus said, "A city being built on a high mountain and fortified cannot fail, nor can it be hidden."

(33) Jesus said, "Preach from your housetops that which you will hear in your ear [(and) in the other ear]. For no one lights a lmap and puts it under a

bushel, nor does he put it in a hidden place, but rather he sets it on a lampstand so that everyone who enters and leaves will see its light."

(34) Jesus said, "If a blind man leads a blind man, they will both fall into a pit."

(35) Jesus said, "It is not possible for anyone to enter the house of a strong man and take it by force unless he binds his hands; then he will (be able to) ransack his house."

(36) Jesus said, "Do not be concerned from morning until evening and from evening until morning about what you will wear."

(37) His disciples said, "When will You become revealed to us and when shall we see You?"

Jesus said, "When you disrobe without being ashamed and take up your garments and place them under your feet like little children and tread on them, then [will you see] the Son of the Living One, and you will not be afraid."

(38) Jesus said, "Many times have you desired to hear these words which I am saying to you, and you have no one else to hear them from. There will be days when you will look for Me and will not find Me."

(39) Jesus said, "The Pharisees and the scribes have taken the keys of Knowledge and hidden them. They themselves have not entered, nor have they allowed to enter those who wish to. You, however, be as wise as serpents and as innocent as doves."

(40) Jesus said, "A grapevine has been planted outside of the Father, but being unsound, it will be pulled up by its roots and destroyed."

(41) Jesus said, "Whoever has something in his hand will receive more, and whoever has nothing will be deprived of even the little he has."

(42) Jesus said, "Become passers-by."

(43) His disciples said to him, "Who are You, that You should say these things to us?"

[Jesus said to them,] "You do not realize who I am from what I say to you, but you have become like the Jews, for they (either) love the tree and hate its fruit (or) love the fruit and hate the tree."

(44) Jesus said, "Whoever blasphemes against the Father will be forgiven, and whoever blasphemes against the Son will be forgiven, but whoever blasphemes against the Holy Spirit will not be forgiven either on earth or in heaven."

(45) Jesus said, "Grapes are not harvested from thorns, nor are figs gathered from thistles, for they do not produce fruit. A good man brings forth good from his storehouse; an evil man brings forth evil things from his evil storehouse which is in his heart, and says evil things. For out of the abun-

dance of the heart he brings forth evil things."

(46) Jesus said, "Among those born of women, from Adam until John the Baptist, there is no one so superior to John the Baptist that his eyes should not be lowered (before him). Yet I have said, whichever one of you comes to be a child will be acquainted with the Kingdom and will become superior to John."

(47) Jesus said, "It is impossible for a man to mount two horses or to stretch two bows. And it is impossible for a servant to serve two masters; otherwise, he will honor the one and treat the other contemptuously. No man drinks old wine and immediately desires to drink new wine. And new wine is not put into old wineskins, lest they burst; nor is old wine put into new wineskin, lest it spoil it. An old patch is not sewn onto a new garment, because a tear would result."

(48) Jesus said, "If two make peace with each other in this one house, they will say to the mountain, 'Move away,' and it will move away."

(49) Jesus said, "Blessed are the solitary and elect, for you will find the Kingdom. For you are from it, and to it you will return."

(50) Jesus said, "If they say to you, 'Where did you come from?', say to them, 'We came from the light, the place where the light came into being on its own accord and established [itself] and became manifest through their image.' If they say to you, 'Is it you?', say, 'We are its children, and we are the elect of the Living Father.' If they ask you, 'What is the sign of your Father in you?', say to them, 'It is movement and repose."

(51) His disciples said to Him, "When will the repose of the dead come about, and when will the new world come?"

He said to them, "What you look forward to has already come, but you do not recognize it."

(52) His disciples said to Him, "Twenty-four prophets spoke in Israel, and all of them spoke in You."

He said to them, "You have omitted the one living in your presence and have spoken (only) of the dead."

(53) His disciples said to Him, "Is circumcision beneficial or not?"

He said to them, "If it were beneficial, their father would beget them already circumcised from their mother. Rather, the true circumcision in spirit has become completely profitable."

(54) Jesus said, "Blessed are the poor for yours is the Kingdom of Heaven."

(55) Jesus said, "Whoever does not hate his father and mother cannot become a disciple to Me. And whoever does not hate his brothers and sisters

and take up his cross in My way will not be worthy of Me."

(56) Jesus said, "Whoever has come to understand the world has found (only) a corpse, and whoever has found a corpse is superior to the world."

(57) Jesus said, "The Kingdom of the Father is like a man who had [good] seed. His enemy came by night and sowed weeds among the good seed. The man did not allow them to pull up the weeds; he said to them, 'I am afraid that you will go intending to pull up the weeds and pull up the wheat along with them.' For on the day of the harvest the weeds will be plainly visible, and they will be pulled up and burned."

(58) Jesus said, "Blessed is the man who has suffered and found life."

(59) Jesus said, "Take heed of the Living One while you are alive, lest you die and seek to see Him and be unable to do so."

(60) [They saw] a Samaritan carrying a lamb on his way to Judea. He said to his disciples, "[Why does] that man [carry] the lamb around?"

They said to Him, "So that he may kill it and eat it."

He said to them, "You too, look for a place for yourselves within Repose, lest you become a corpse and be eaten."

(61) Jesus said, "Two will rest on a bed: the one will die, and [the] other will live."

Salome said, "Who are You, man, that You, as though from the One, (or: as [whose son] that You) have come up on my couch and eaten from my table?"

Jesus said to her, "I am He who exists from the Undivided. I was given some of the things of My father."

[Salome said,] "I am Your disciple."

[Jesus said to her,] "Therefore I say, if he is [undivided], he will be filled with light, but if he is divided, he will be filled with darkness."

(62) Jesus said, "It is to those [who are worthy of My] mysteries that I tell My mysteries. Do not let your left hand know what your right hand is doing."

(63) Jesus said, "There was a rich man who had much money. He said, 'I shall put my money to use so that I may sow, reap, plant, and fill my store-house with produce, with the result that I shall lack nothing.' Such were his intentions, but that same night he died. Let him who has ears hear."

(64) Jesus said, "A man had received visitors. And when he had prepared the dinner, he sent his servant to invite the guests. He went to the first one and said to him, 'My master invites you.' He said, 'I have claims against some merchants. They are coming to me this evening. I must go and give them my orders. I ask to be excused from the dinner.' He went to another and said to him, 'My master has invited you.' He said to him, 'I have just bought a house

and am required for the day. I shall not have any spare time.' He went to another and said to him, 'My master invites you.' He said to him, 'My friend is going to get married, and I am to prepare the banquet. I shall not be able to come. I ask to be excused from the dinner.' He went to another and said to him, 'My master invites you.' He said to him, 'I have just bought a farm, and I am on my way to collect the rent. I shall not be able to come. I ask to be excused.' The servant returned and said to his master, 'Those whom you invited to the dinner have asked to be excused.' The master said to his servant, 'Go outside to the streets and bring back those whom you happen to meet, so that they may dine.' Businessmen and merchants will not enter the Places of My Father."

(65) He said, "There was a good man who owned a vineyard. He leased it to tenant farmers so that they might work it and he might collect the produce from them. He sent his servant so that the tenants might give him the produce of the vineyard. They seized his servant and beat him, all but killing him. The servant went back and told his master. The master said, 'Perhaps [they] did not recognize [him].' He sent another servant. The tenants beat this one as well. Then the owner sent his son and said, 'Perhaps they will show respect to my son.' Because the tenants knew that it was he who was the heir to the vineyard, they seized him and killed him. Let him who has ears hear."

(66) Jesus said, "Show me the stone which the builders have rejected. That one is the cornerstone."

(67) Jesus said, "Whoever believes that the All itself is deficient is (himself) completely deficient."

(68) Jesus said, "Blessed are you when you are hated and persecuted. Wherever you have been persecuted they will find no Place."

(69) Jesus said, "Blessed are they who have been persecuted within themselves. It is they who have truly come to know the Father. Blessed are the hungry, for the belly of him who desires will be filled."

(70) Jesus said, "That which you have will save you if you bring it forth from yourselves. That which you do not have within you will kill you if you do not have it within you."

(71) Jesus said, "I shall destroy [this] house, and no one will be able to rebuild it."

(72) [A man said] to Him, "Tell my brothers to divide my father's possessions with me."

He said to him, "O man, who has made Me a divider?"

He turned to His disciples and said to them, "I am not a divider, am I?"

(73) Jesus said, "The harvest is great but the laborers are few. Beseech the

Lord, therefore, to send out laborers to the harvest."

(74) He said, "O Lord, there are many around the drinking trough, but there is nothing in the cistern."

(75) Jesus said, "Many are standing at the door, but it is the solitary who will enter the bridal chamber."

(76) Jesus said, "The Kingdom of the Father is like a merchant who had a consignment of merchandise and who discovered a pearl. That merchant was shrewd. He sold the merchandise and bought the pearl alone for himself. You too, seek his unfailing and enduring treasure where no moth comes near to devour and no worm destroys."

(77) Jesus said, "It is I who am the light which is above them all. It is I whom am the All. From Me did the All come forth, and unto Me did the All extend. Split a piece of wood, and I am there. Lift up the stone, and you will find Me there."

(78) Jesus said, "Why have you come out into the desert? To see a reed shaken by the wind? And to see a man clothed in fine garments like your kings and your great men? Upon them are the fine [garments], and they are unable to discern the truth."

(79) A woman from the crowd said to Him, "Blessed are the womb which bore You and the breasts which nourished You."

He said to her, "Blessed are those who have heard the word of the Father and have truly kept it. For there will be days when you will say, 'Blessed are the womb which has not conceived and the breasts which have not given milk.'"

(80) Jesus said, "He who has recognized the world has found the body, but he who has found the body is superior to the world."

(81) Jesus said, "Let him who has grown rich be king, and let him who possesses power renounce it."

(82) Jesus said, "He who is near Me is near the fire, and he who is far from Me is far from the Kingdom."

(83) Jesus said, "The images are manifest to man, but the light in them remains concealed in the image of the light of the Father. He will become manifest, but his image will remain concealed by his light."

(84) Jesus said, "When you see your likeness, you rejoice. But when you see your images which came into being before you, and which neither die nor become manifest, how much will you have to bear!"

(85) Jesus said, "Adam came into being from a great power and a great wealth, but he did not become worthy of you. For had he been worthy, [he would] not [have experienced] death."

(86) Jesus said, "[The foxes have their holes] and the birds have [their] nests, but the Son of Man has no place to lay his head and rest."

(87) Jesus said, "Wretched is the body that is dependent upon a body, and wretched is the soul that is dependent on these two."

(88) Jesus said, "The angels and the prophets will come to you and give to you those things you (already) have. And you too, give them those things which you have, and say to yourselves, "When will they come and take what is theirs?""

(89) Jesus said, "Why do you wash the outside of the cup? Do you not realize that he who made the inside is the same one who made the outside?"

(90) Jesus said, "Come unto me, for My yoke is easy and My lordship is mild, and you will find repose for yourselves."

(91) They said to Him, "Tell us who You are so that we may believe in You."

He said to them, "You read the face of the sky and of the earth, but you have not recognized the one who (or: that which) is before you, and you do not know how to read this moment."

(92) Jesus said, "Seek and you will find. Yet, what you asked Me about in former times and which I did not tell you then, now I do desire to tell, but you do not inquire after it."

(93) [Jesus said,] "Do not give what is holy to dogs, lest they throw them on the dung-heap. Do not throw the pearls to swine, lest they grind it [to bits]."

(94) Jesus [said], "If you have money, do not lend it at interest, but give [it] to one from whom you will not get it back."

(96) Jesus [said], "The Kingdom of the Father is like a certain woman. She took a little leaven, [concealed] it in some dough, and made it into larger loaves. Let him who has ears hear."

(97) Jesus said, "The Kingdom of the [Father] is like a certain woman who was carrying a jar full of meal. While she was walking [on] a road, still some distance from home, the handle of the jar broke and the meal emptied out behind her on the road. She did not realize it; she had noticed no accident. When she reached her house, she set the jar down and found it empty."

(98) Jesus said, "The Kingdom of the Father is like a certain man who wanted to kill a powerful man. In his own house he drew his sword and stuck it into the wall in order to find out whether his hand could carry through. Then he slew the powerful man."

(99) The disciples said to Him, "Your brothers and Your mother are

standing outside."

He said to them, "Those here who do the will of My Father are My brothers and My mother. It is they who will enter the Kingdom of My Father."

(100) They showed Jesus a gold coin and said to Him, "Caesar's men demand taxes from us."

(101) [Jesus said,] "Whoever does not hate his father and his mother as I do cannot become a disciple to Me. And whoever does [not] love his father and his mother as I do cannot become a [disciple] to me. For My mother [gave me falsehood], but [My] true [Mother] gave me life."

(102) Jesus said, "Woe to the Pharisees, for they are like a dog sleeping in the manger of oxen, for neither does he eat nor does he let the oxen eat."

(103) Jesus said, "Fortunate is the man who knows where the brigands will enter, so that he may get up, muster his domain, and arm himself before they invade."

(104) They said [to Jesus], "Come, let us pray today and let us fast."

Jesus said, "What is the sin that I have committed, or wherein have I been defeated? But when the bridegroom leaves the bridal chamber, then let them fast and pray."

(105) Jesus said, "He who knows the father and the mother will be called the son of a harlot."

(106) Jesus said, "When you make the two one, you will become the sons of man, and when you say, 'Mountain, move away,' it will move away."

(107) Jesus said, "The Kingdom is like a shepherd who had a hundred sheep. One of them, the largest, went astray. He left the ninety-nine and looked for that one until he found it. When he had gone to such trouble, he said to the sheep, 'I care for you more than the ninety-nine.'"

(108) Jesus said, "He who will drink from My mouth will become like Me. I myself shall become he, and the things that are hidden will be revealed to him."

(109) Jesus said, "The Kingdom is like a man who had a [hidden] treasure in his field without knowing it. And [after] he died, he left it to his son. The son did not know (about the treasure). He inherited the field and sold [it]. And the one who bought it went plowing and found the treasure. He began to lend money at interest to whomever he wished.

(110) Jesus said, "Whoever finds the world and becomes rich, let him renounce the world."

(111) Jesus said, "The heavens and the earth will be rolled up in your presence. And the one who lives from the Living One will not see death. Does

not Jesus say, "Whoever finds himself is superior to the world"?

(112) Jesus said, "Woe to the flesh that depends on the soul; woe to the soul that depends on the flesh."

(113) His disciples said to Him, "When will the Kingdom come?"

[Jesus said,] "It will not come by waiting for it. It will not be a matter of saying 'Here it is' or 'There it is.' Rather, the Kingdom of the Father is spread out upon the earth, and men do not see it."

(114) Simon Peter said to them, "Let Mary leave us, for women are not worthy of Life."

Jesus said, "I myself shall lead her in order to make her male, so that she too may become a living spirit resembling you males. For every woman who will make herself male will enter the Kingdom of Heaven."[9]

"Q"

It has long been theorized that before the written gospels came into existence, collections of sayings of Jesus circulated independently. At first, the theory goes, these sayings were transmitted orally, undergoing progressive alteration but remaining faithful to the language used by Jesus. With the passage of time, certain sayings were written down chiefly as an *aide memoire* for missionaries, faced with the task of teaching, converting, and settling disputes in individual Christian communities. A first-century bishop, Papias of Hierapolis, encourages this theory in his testimony concerning the origin of an Aramaic "gospel" of Matthew (which bears no resemblance to the gospel of that name in the New Testament). According to Papias, Matthew "composed the sayings of the Lord in Hebrew," and others made use of them as they chose. Lacking any such sayings collection, it is impossible to know if the canonical Gospels were indeed formed by the process of extraction which Papias describes.

The discovery of the Gnostic sayings-gospel, *The Gospel of Thomas*, does not necessarily provide evidence of these early collections, since it *presupposes* the existence of the Canonical Gospels and presents its sayings in the form of revealer-discourses and aphorisms without any pretense of historicity. Moreover, given the increasingly spiritual interpretation of Jesus in the early church, it is not clear why sayings-collections of the revealer-discourse variety would have fallen into disuse.

Even in the face of bad and paltry evidence, the sayings-source theory has achieved remarkable acceptance among scholars, largely, one suspects, because it is very difficult to embrace the conclusions that the "radical" Dutch School of New Testament critics arrived at toward the beginning of this century: that no saying of Jesus recorded in the New Testament can be considered genuine, each and every one arising out of Christian missionary propaganda. By the time Jesus' prominence was such that a record of his teachings was considered necessary, the Dutch scholars argued, no record was possible.[10] Ironically, this was so because the very stature that invested his teachings with authority actually determined the *substance* of the sayings attributed to him by the early believers.

Those who still cling to the postulate of a sayings-source point to a kind of ersatz-evidence in its favor: There are passages in the Synoptic Gospels where Matthew and Luke show a close resemblance to each other but not to anything in Mark. This large parcel of material consists almost entirely of sayings of Jesus, though it includes other material as well (for example, on John the Baptist, the healing of the centurion's son, and the account of the temptation).

Based on a close consideration of the relationship between Matthew and Luke, including especially the respective arrangement of common material and their selective "disuse" of Mark, a number of scholars concluded (1) that Matthew and Luke had independent access to a collection of sayings of Jesus, written in Greek; (2) that its whole content was used either by Matthew or Luke, or both; and (3) that the order of contents in Luke is nearer to the original written source than in Matthew. To this document, scholars gave the name "Q," from the initial of the German word *Quelle* (source).[11] The existence of "Q" is hotly contested[12]—to many it seems a convenience rather than a solution to the so-called synoptic problem—but no consideration of the sayings-tradition would be complete without it.

The following reconstruction of "Q" is based on the Lucan version (New English Bible translation). The sixty-six literary units (pericopes) given here include a variety of forms: narrative material, parables and oracles, beatitudes and woes, wisdom-pronouncements, and exhortations. All of these forms are permeated, however, by a strong eschatological emphasis. Luke 7:2-10 (= Matt 8:5-13) is not given here, though it is sometimes assigned to the "Q"-document.

1. He said to them: "You vipers' brood! Who warned you to escape from the coming retribution? Then prove your repentance by the fruit it bears; and do not begin saying to yourselves, 'We have Abraham for our father.' I tell you that God can make children for Abraham out of these stones here. Already the axe is laid to the roots of the trees; and every tree that fails to produce good fruit is cut down and thrown on the fire."

2. He spoke out and said to them all: "I baptize you with water; but there is one to come who is mightier than I. I am not fit to unfasten his shoes. He will baptize you with the Holy Spirit and with fire. His shovel is ready in his hand, to winnow his threshing-floor and gather the wheat into his granary; but he will burn the chaff on a fire that can never go out."

3. The devil said to him, "If you are the Son of God, tell this stone to become bread." Jesus answered, "Scripture says, 'Man cannot live on bread alone.'"

Next the devil led him up and showed him in a flash all the kingdoms of the world. "All this dominion will I give to you," he said, "and the glory that goes with it; for it has been put in my hands and I can give it to anyone I choose. You have only to do homage to me and it shall all be yours." Jesus answered him, "Scripture says, 'You shall do homage to the Lord your God and worship him alone.'"

The devil took him to Jerusalem and set him on the parapet of the temple. "If you are the Son of God," he said, "throw yourself down; for Scripture says, 'He will give his angels orders to take care of you,' and again, 'They will support you in their arms for fear you should strike your foot against a stone.'" Jesus answered him, "It has been said, 'You are not to put the Lord your God to the test.'"

4. Turning to his disciples he began to speak:

"How blest are you are in need; the kingdom of God is yours.

"How blest are you who now go hungry; your hunger shall be satisfied.

"How blest are you who weep now; you shall laugh.

"How blest are you when men hate, when they outlaw you and insult you, and ban your very name as infamous, because of the Son of Man. On that day be glad and dance for joy; for assuredly you have a rich reward in heaven;

in just the same way did their fathers treat the prophets.

5. "But to you who hear me I say:

"Love your enemies; do good to those who hate you; bless those who curse you; pray for those who treat you spitefully. When a man hits you on the cheek, offer him the other cheek too; when a man takes your coat, let him have your shirt as well. Give to everyone who asks you; when a man takes what is yours, do not demand it back. Treat others as you would like them to treat you.

6. "If you love only those who love you, what credit is that to you? Even sinners love those who love them. Again, if you do good only to those who do good to you, what credit is that to you? Even sinners do as much. And if you lend only where you expect to be repaid, what credit is that to you? Even sinners lend to each other to be repaid in full. But you must love your enemies and do good; and lend without expecting any return; and you will have a rich reward: you will be sons of the Most High, because he himself is kind to the ungrateful and wicked. Be compassionate as your Father is compassionate.

7. "Pass no judgment, and you will not be judged; do not condemn, and you will not be condemned; acquit, and you will be acquitted; give, and gifts will be given you. Good measure, pressed down, shaken together, and running over, will be poured into your lap; for whatever measure you deal out to others will be dealt to you in return."

8. He also offered them a parable: "Can one blind man be guide to another? Will they not both fall into the ditch? A pupil is not superior to his teacher; but everyone, when his training is complete, will reach his teacher's level.

"Why do you look at the speck of sawdust in your brother's eye, with never a thought for the great plank in your own? How can you say to your brother, 'My dear brother, let me take the speck out of your eye,' when you are blind to the plank in your own? You hypocrite! First take the plank out of your own eye, and then you will see clearly to take the speck out of your brother's.

9. "There is no such thing as a good tree producing worthless fruit, nor yet a worthless tree producing good fruit. For each tree is known by its own fruit: you do not gather figs from thistles, and you do not pick grapes from brambles. A good man produces good from the store of good within himself; and an evil man from evil within produces evil. For the words that the mouth utters come from the overflowing of the heart.

10. "Why do you keep calling me 'Lord, Lord'—and never do what I tell you? Everyone who comes to me and hears what I say, and acts upon it—I

will show you what he is like. He is like a man who, in building his house, dug deep and laid the foundations on rock. When the flood came, the river burst upon that house, but could not shift it, because it had been soundly built. But he who hears and does not act is like a man who built his house on the soil without foundations. As soon as the river burst upon it, the house collapsed, and fell with a great crash."

11. "Go," he said, "and tell John what you have seen and heard: how the blind recover their sight, the lame walk, the lepers are made clean, the deaf hear, the dead are raised to life, the poor are hearing the good news—and happy is the man who does not find me a stumbling-block."

12. Jesus began to speak about him to the crowds: "What was the spectacle that drew you to the wilderness? A reed-bed swept by the wind? No? Then what did you go out to see? A man dressed in silks and satins? Surely you must look in palaces for great clothes and luxury. But what did you go out to see? A prophet? Yes indeed, and far more than a prophet. He is the man of whom Scripture says,

'Here is my herald, whom I send on ahead of you,
    and he will prepare your way before you.'
I tell you, there is not a mother's son greater than John, and yet the least in the kingdom of God is greater than he."

13. "How can I describe the people of this generation? What are they like? They are like children sitting in the market-place and shouting at each other,

'We piped for you and you would not dance.
We wept and wailed, and you would not mourn.'

For John the Baptist came neither eating bread nor drinking wine, and you say, 'He is possessed.' The Son of Man came eating and drinking, and you say, 'Look at him! a glutton and a drinker, a friend of tax-gatherers and sinners!' And yet God's wisdom is proved right by all who are her children."

14. A man said to him, "I will follow you wherever you go." Jesus answered, "Foxes have their holes, the birds their roosts; but the Son of Man has nowhere to lay his head."

15. "Follow me," but the man replied, "Let me go and bury my father first." Jesus said, "Leave the dead to bury their dead; you must go and announce the kingdom of God."

16. He said to them: "The crop is heavy, but laborers are scarce; you must therefore beg the owner to send laborers to harvest his crop. Be on your way. And look, I am sending you like lambs among wolves. Carry no purse

or pack, and travel barefoot. Exchange no greetings on the road. When you go into a house, let your first words be, 'Peace to this house.' If there is a man of peace there, your peace will rest upon him; if not, it will return and rest upon you. Stay in that one house, sharing their food and drink; for the worker earns his pay. Do not move from house to house. When you come into a town and they make you welcome, eat the food provided for you; heal the sick there, and say, 'The kingdom of God has come close to you.' When you enter a town and they do not make you welcome, go out into its streets and say, 'The very dust of your town that clings to our feet we wipe off to your shame. Only take note of this: the kingdom of God has come close.' I tell you, it will be more bearable for Sodom on the great Day than for that town.

17. "Alas for you, Chorazin! Alas for you, Bethsaida! If the miracles that were performed in you had been performed in Tyre and Sidon, they would have repented long ago, sitting in sackcloth and ashes. But it will be more bearable for Tyre and Sidon at the Judgment than for you. And as for you, Capernaum, will you be exalted to the skies? No, brought down to the depths!

18. "Whoever listens to you listens to me; whoever rejects you rejects me. And whoever rejects me rejects the One who sent me.

19. "I thank thee, Father, Lord of heaven and earth, for hiding these things from the learned and wise, and revealing them to the simple. Yes, Father, such was thy choice."

20. Then turning to his disciples he said, "Everything is entrusted to me by my Father; and no one knows who the Son is but the Father, or who the Father is but the Son, and those to whom the Son may choose to reveal him."

21. Turning to his disciples in private he said, "Happy the eyes that see what you are seeing! I tell you, many prophets and kings wished to see what you now see, yet never saw it; to hear what you hear, yet never heard it."

22. He answered, "When you pray, say,

> 'Father, thy name be hallowed;
> thy kingdom come.
> Give us each day our daily bread.
> And forgive us our sins,
> for we too forgive all who have done us wrong.
> And do not bring us to the test.'"

23. "I say to you, ask, and you will receive; seek, and you will find; knock, and the door will be opened. For everyone who asks receives, he who seeks finds, and to him who knocks, the door will be opened.

24. "Is there a father among you who will not offer his son a snake when he

asks for fish, or a scorpion when he asks for an egg? If you, then, bad as you are, know how to give your children what is good for them, how much more will the heavenly Father give the Holy Spirit to those who ask him!"

25. But he knew what was in their minds, and said, "Every kingdom divided against itself goes to ruin, and a divided household falls. Equally if Satan is divided against himself, how can his kingdom stand?—since, as you would have it, I drive out the devils by Beelzebub. If it is by Beelzebub that I cast out devils, by whom do your own people drive them out? If this is your argument, they themselves will refute you. But if it is by the finger of God that I drive out the devils, then be sure the kingdom of God has already come upon you.

26. "When an unclean spirit comes out of a man it wanders over the deserts seeking a resting-place; and if it finds none, it says, 'I will go back to the home I left.' So it returns and finds the house swept clean, and tidy. Off it goes and collects seven other spirits more wicked than itself, and they all come in and settle down; and in the end the man's plight is worse than before.

27. "The only sign that will be given it is the sign of Jonah. For just as Jonah was a sign to the Ninevites, so will the Son of Man be to this generation. At the Judgment, when the men of this generation are on trial, the Queen of the South will appear against them and ensure their condemnation, for she came from the ends of the earth to hear the wisdom of Solomon; and what is here is greater than Solomon. The men of Nineveh will appear at the Judgment when this generation is on trial, and ensure its condemnation, for they repented at the preaching of Jonah; and what is here is greater than Jonah.

28. "No one lights a lamp and puts it in a cellar, but rather on the lampstand so that those who enter may see the light. The lamp of your body is the eye. When you eyes are sound, you have light for your whole body; but when the eyes are bad, you are in darkness. See to it then that the light you have is not darkness. If you have light for your whole body with no trace of darkness, it will be as bright as when a lamp flashes its rays upon you.

29. The Lord said to him, "You Pharisees! You clean the outside of cup and plate; but inside you there is nothing but greed and wickedness. You fools! Did not he who made the outside make the inside too?

30. "Alas for you Pharisees! You pay tithes of mint and rue and every garden-herb, but have no care for justice and the love of God. It is these you should have practiced, without neglecting the others.

31. "Alas for you Pharisees! You love the seats of honor in synagogues, and salutations in the marketplaces.

32. "Yes, you lawyers, it is no better with you! For you load men with intolerable burdens, and will not put a single finger to the load.

33. "Alas, you build the tombs of the prophets whom your fathers murdered, and so testify that you approve of the deeds your fathers did; they committed the murders and you provide the tombs.

34. "This is why the Wisdom of God said, 'I will send them prophets and messengers; and some of these they will persecute and kill'; so that this generation will have to answer for the blood of all the prophets shed since the foundation of the world; from the blood of Abel to the blood of Zechariah who perished between the altar and the sanctuary. I tell you, this generation will have to answer for it all.

35. "Alas for you lawyers! You have taken away the key of knowledge. You did not go in yourselves, and those who were on their way in, you stopped.

36. "There is nothing covered up that will not be uncovered, nothing hidden that will not be made known. You may take it, then, that everything you have said in the dark will be heard in broad daylight, and what you have whispered behind closed doors will be shouted from the house-tops.

37. "To you who are my friends I say: Do not fear those who will kill the body and after that have nothing more they can do. I will warn you whom to fear: fear him who, after he has killed, has authority to cast into hell. Believe me, he is the one to fear.

38. "Are not sparrows five for twopence? And yet no one of them is overlooked by God. More than that, even the hairs of your head have all been counted. Have no fear; you are worth more than any number of sparrows.

39. "I tell you this: Everyone who acknowledges me before men, the Son of Man will acknowledge before the angels of God; but he who disowns me before men will be disowned before the angels of God.

40. "Anyone who speaks a word against the Son of Man will receive forgiveness; but for him who slanders the Holy Spirit there will be no forgiveness.

41. "When you are brought before synagogues and state authorities, do not begin worrying about how you will conduct your defence or what you will say. For when the time comes the Holy Spirit wil instruct you what to say.

42. "Therefore," he said to his disciples, "I bid you to put away anxious thoughts about food to keep you alive and clothes to cover your body. Life is more than food, the body more than clothes. Think of the ravens: they neither sow nor reap; they have no storehouse or barn; yet God feeds them. You are

worth far more than the birds! Is there a man among you who by anxious thought can add a foot to his height? If, then, you cannot do even a very little thing, why are you anxious about the rest?

43. "Think of the lilies: they neither spin nor weave; yet I tell you, even Solomon in all his splendour was not attired like one of these. But if that is how God clothes the grass, which is growing in the field today, and tomorrow is thrown on the stove, how much more will he clothe you! How little faith you have! And so you are not to set your mind on food and drink; you are not to worry. For all these are things for the heathen to run after; but you have a Father who knows that you need them. No, set your mind upon his kingdom, and all the rest will come to you as well.

43a. "Provide for yourselves purses that do not wear out, and never-failing treasure in heaven, where no thief can get near it, no moth destroy it. For where your treasure is, there will your heart be also.

44. "And remember, if the householder had known what time the burglar was coming he would not have let his house be broken into. Hold yourselves ready, then, because the Son of Man will come at the time you least expect him."

45. The Lord said, "Well, who is the trusty and sensible man whom his master will appoint as his steward, to manage his servants and issue their rations at the proper time? Happy that servant who is found at his task when his master comes! I tell you this: He will be put in charge of all his master's property. But if that servant says to himself, 'The master is a long time coming,' and begins to bully the menservants and maids, and eat and drink and get drunk; then the master will arrive on a day that servant does not expect, at a time he does not know, and will cut him in pieces. Thus he will find his place among the faithless.

46. "Do you suppose I came to establish peace on earth? No indeed, I have come to bring division. For from now on, five members of a family will be divided, three against two and two against three; father against son and son against father, mother against daughter and daughter against mother, mother against son's wife and son's wife against her mother-in-law."

47. He also said to the people, "When you see cloud banking up in the west, you say at once, 'It is going to rain,' and rain it does. And when the wind is from the south, you say, 'There will be a heat-wave,' and there is. What hypocrites you are! You know how to interpret the appearance of earth and sky; how is it you cannot interpret this fateful hour?

48. "And why can you not judge for yourselves what is the right course? When you are going with your opponent to court, make an effort to settle

with him while you are still on the way; otherwise he may drag you before the judge, and the judge hand you over to the constable, and the constable put you in jail. I tell you, you will not come out till you have paid the last farthing."

49. Again he said, "The kingdom of God, what shall I compare it with? It is like the yeast which a woman took and mixed with half a hundredweight of flour till it was all leavened.

50. "Struggle to get in through the narrow door; for I tell you that many will try to enter and not be able.

51. "When once the master of the house has got up and locked the door, you may stand outside and knock, and say, 'Sir, let us in!' but he will only answer, 'I do not know where you come from.' Then you will begin to say, 'We sat at table with you and you taught in our streets.' But he will repeat, 'I tell you, I do not know where you come from. Out of my sight, all of you, you and your wicked ways!'

52. "There will be wailing and grinding of teeth here, when you see Abraham, Isaac, and Jacob, and all the prophets, in the kingdom of God, and yourselves thrown out. From east and west people will come, from north and south, for the feast in the kingdom of God.

53. "O Jerusalem, Jerusalem, the city that murders the prophets and stones the messengers sent to her! How often have I longed to gather your children, as a hen gathers her brood under her wings; but you would not let me. Look, look! there is your temple, forsaken by God. And I tell you, you shall never see me until the time comes when you say, 'Blessings on him who comes in the name of the Lord!'"

54. Jesus answered, "A man was giving a big dinner party and had sent out many invitations. At dinnertime he sent his servant with a message for his guests, 'Please come, everything is now ready.' They began one and all to excuse themselves. The first said, 'I have bought a piece of land, and I must go and look over it; please accept my apologies.' The second said, 'I have bought five yoke of oxen, and I am on my way to try them out; please accept my apologies.' The next said, 'I have just got married and for that reason I cannot come.' When the servant came back he reported this to his master. The master of the house was angry and said to him, 'Go out quickly into the streets and alleys of the town, and bring me in the poor, the crippled, the blind, and the lame.' The servant said, 'Sir, your orders have been carried out and there is still room.' The master replied, 'Go out on to the highways and along the hedgerows and make them come in; I want my house to be full. I tell you that not one of those who were invited shall taste my banquet.'

55. "If anyone comes to me and does not hate his father and mother, wife and children, brothers and sisters, even his own life, he cannot be a disciple of mine. No one who does not carry his cross and come with me can be a disciple of mine."

56. He answered them with this parable: "If one of you has a hundred sheep and loses one of them, does he not leave the ninety-nine in the open pasture and go after the missing one until he has found it? How delighted he is then! He lifts it on his shoulders, and home he goes to call his friends and neighbors together. 'Rejoice with me!' he cries. 'I have found my lost sheep.' In the same way, I tell you, there will be greater joy in heaven over one sinner who repents than over ninety-nine righteous people who do not need to repent.

57. "No servant can be the slave of two masters; for either he will hate the first and love the second, or he will be devoted to the first and think nothing of the second. You cannot serve God and Money.

58. "Until John, it was the Law and the prophets: since then, there is the good news of the kingdom of God, and everyone forces his way in.

59. "It is easier for heaven and earth to come to an end than for one dot or stroke of the Law to lose its force.

60. "Keep watch on yourselves. If your brother wrongs you, reprove him; and if he repents, forgive him. Even if he wrongs you seven times in a day and comes back to you seven times saying, 'I am sorry,' you are to forgive him."

61. The apostles said to the Lord, "Increase our faith"; and the Lord replied, "If you had faith no bigger than a mustard-seed, you could say to this mulberry-tree, 'Be rooted and replanted in the sea'; and it would at once obey you."

62. He said to the disciples, "The time will come when you will long to see one of the days of the Son of Man, but you will not see it. They will say to you 'Look! There!' and 'Look! Here!' Do not go running off in pursuit. For like the lightning-flash that lights up the earth from end to end, will the Son of Man be when his day comes. But first he must endure much suffering and be repudiated by this generation.

63. "As things were in Noah's days, so will they be in the days of the Son of Man. They ate and drank and married, until the day that Noah went into the ark and the flood came and made an end of them all. As things were in Lot's days, also; they ate and drank; they bought and sold; they planted and built; but the day that Lot went out from Sodom, it rained fire and sulphur from the sky and made an end of them all—it will be like that on the day when the Son of Man is revealed.

64. "On that day the man who is on the roof and his belongings in the house must not come down to pick them up; he, too, who is in the fields must not go back. Remember Lot's wife. Whoever seeks to save his life will lose it; and whoever loses it will save it, and live.

65. "I tell you, on that night there will be two men in one bed: one will be taken, the other left. There will be two women together grinding corn: one will be taken, the other left." When they heard this they asked, "Where, Lord?" He said, "Where the corpse is, there the vultures will gather."

66. He said, "A man of noble birth went on a long journey abroad, to be appointed king and then return . . . Back he came as king, and sent for the servants to whom he had given the money, to see what profit each had made. The first came and said, 'Your pound, sir, has made ten more.' 'Well done,' he replied, 'you are a good servant. You have shown yourself trustworthy in a very small matter, and you will have charge of ten cities.' The second came and said, 'Your pound, sir, has made five more,' and he also was told, 'You too, take charge of five cities.' The third came and said, 'Here is your pound, sir; I kept it put away in a handkerchief. I was afraid of you, because you are a hard man: you draw out what you never put in and reap what you did not sow.' 'You rascal!' he replied; 'I will judge you by your own words. You knew, did you, that I am a hard man, that I draw out what I never put in, and reap what I did not sow? Then why did you not put my money on deposit, so I could have claimed it with interest when I came back?' Turning to his attendants he said, 'Take the pound from him and give it to the man with ten.' 'But sir,' they replied, 'he has ten already.' 'I tell you,' he went on, 'the man who has will always be given more; but the man who has not will forfeit even what he has.'"

Four

THE GROWTH OF THE JESUS MYTH: APOCRYPHAL GOSPELS

The canonical Gospels represent only a fraction of those produced in early Christianity. Writing toward the end of the first century, the author of the Gospel of Luke speaks (1:1-4) of the "many writers who have undertaken to draw up accounts" of the events concerning Jesus. Though we cannot be sure precisely what these "other" gospels looked like, it is probable that many contained no more than an account of the passion and death of Jesus, followed by a simple statement concerning the resurrection.

As the earliest manuscripts of Mark's Gospel ended at 16:8 ("They went out and ran away from the tomb, beside themselves with terror. They said nothing to anybody, for they were afraid"), it is clear that the first *expansions* of the passion-story were additions to the legend of Jesus' resurrection (for example, Mark 16:9-20; the special material in Luke 24; and the entirety of chapter 28 in Matthew). These early accounts are contradictory at almost every turn; in the case of Mark's Gospel alone, at least two entirely different resurrection stories have been woven together (16:1-8a, 16:9-20) with very little skill. The Gospel of John offers still other accounts (John 20:1-31; 21:1-25).

Gnostic Christians were especially fond of inventing resurrection stories, finding long discourses by the risen Christ an obvious vehicle for their antimaterialistic philosophy. Indeed, the majority of Gnostics, most radically the Basilidean sect, taught that the death of Jesus had been an illusion carried out by the supreme God to trick the Archons—a teaching apparently at issue in the story of "doubting Thomas" (John 20:25-26) and in Luke 24:43, where Jesus eats a fish to prove that he is not merely an apparition or ghost.

Just as the resurrection story served as an appendix to the passion narrative, the original passion-gospel underwent expansion in a forward direction as well. Stories *about* Jesus—his "prophecies" of judgment and return, the fate of cities and nonbelievers, the punishment of the Jews, and his charge to his followers, even such moral teaching as we find in the Gospels—are written with the crucifixion in view. The signs and wonders he performs—to the astonishment of the multitudes—are only secondarily introduced for the purpose of showing Jesus to be a "magician."[1] Their primary purpose is to focus attention on the fact that he is the eschatological Son of Man—the healer and redeemer of Israel.

It was popularly believed that this redeemer would be made known by his ability to perform cures (see Acts 2:22)—or to put it precisely, that his miracles would serve as certification of his identity. Hence the evangelists' emphasis, varying only in degree, on the healings and nature miracles. We can imagine that whole collections of these stories circulated freely in the first and second centuries and that the canonical Gospels incorporate one or more of these sources. The Gospel of John makes use of another miracles collection, wherein the signs (for example, the raising of Lazarus) are more dramatic than those in the Synoptic Gospels.[2]

Finally, and last in terms of composition, the Gospels were supplemented by nativity stories, designed to ensure and to establish the divine origin of Jesus and to propagate the doctrine of virgin birth. This motif is common in Hellinistic literature. We possess stories about the miraculous births of Plato, Alexander the Great, Augustus, and a variety of other notables. The birth narratives of the Gospels of Matthew and Luke belong formally to this common literary tradition.

Outside the canonical Gospels, passion, resurrection, and infancy stories exist which in the main were written to supplement the "official" Gospels. The technical name for this literature is Apocrypha, from the Greek word *apokryphon* (hidden). In fact, these gospels have never been "hidden" in any deliberate way, merely excluded from the recognized scripture of the church. And even while excluded, the church has derived a number of devotional stories from the apocryphal gospels, and freely exploited some of the traditions they embody—especially stories concerning the childhood of Mary and the circumstances of her betrothal to Joseph. For centuries, artists have been attracted by their naiveté and literary innocence.

Although these accounts date from the second century and later, we cannot be certain that they do not draw on traditions of an earlier period. However that may be, the apocryphal gospels cannot be assumed to preserve anything of historical value. They demonstrate the tendency to further mythicize and expand the story of Jesus in the interest of gaining converts, correcting or supplementing the existing Gospels, and even entertaining the curious. It should be stressed that *none of these purposes is missing* in the New Testament, though many scholars are reluctant, even today, to move beyond the tendency to use the canonical Gospels as standards against which to measure the authenticity of the material we find in the excluded writings.

The Gospel of Peter

This gospel, surviving only as a fragment, was discovered in 1886 in Egypt. In its present form, the gospel dates from no earlier than the second century and represents a freewheeling fictional enlargement of the passion narratives contained in the canonical Gospels. There is nothing to be said for the opinion that *The Gospel of Peter* (or part of it) antedates the four gospels of the New Testament or served as a source for their authors. The well-developed hostility toward the Jews in the writing, the favorable view of Pilate, and the reference to Jesus' descent into Hell (10:41), show affinities with the *Acts of Pilate*. The staccato-style of the transitions in *The Gospel of Peter* suggest that it originated as a sermon or catechetical lesson for proselytes.

Especially notable in this gospel (8:28-34) is the elaboration of Matthew 27:62-66 concerning the guard posted outside Jesus' tomb. So as to leave no possible doubt about the resurrection, seven seals are placed on the tomb, the soldiers pitch a tent to keep watch two by two, and crowds from Jerusalem arrive "to see the sepulchre that had been sealed." Two features of this work deserve comment: first, the *Gospel* is designed to sketch in the events transpiring between the crucifixion and the discovery of the empty tomb (see 8:35-10:42), details which the Synoptic Gospels lack. Second, the *Gospel*, though attributed to Peter, is told from an "apostolic" standpoint (14:59) that betrays development of a church hierarchy. In short, the gospel was written at a time when the primacy of Peter was considered a proof of its credibility.

The Gospel of Peter

1:1. But of the Jews none washed their hands, neither Herod nor any one of his judges. And as they would not wash, Pilate arose. **2.** And then Herod the king commanded that the Lord should be marched off, saying to them, "What I have commanded you to do to him, do ye."

2:3. Now there stood there Joseph, the friend of Pilate and of the Lord, and knowing that they were about to crucify him he came to Pilate and begged the body of the Lord for burial. **4.** And Pilate sent to Herod and begged his body. **5.** And Herod said, "Brother Pilate, even if no one had begged him, we should bury him, since the Sabbath is drawing on. For it stands written in the law: the sun should not set on one that has been put to death."

And he delivered him to the people on the day before the unleavened bread, their feast. **3:6.** So they took the Lord and pushed him in great haste and said, "Let us hail the Son of God now that we have gotten power over him." **7.** And they put upon him a purple robe and set him on the judgment seat and said, "Judge righteously, O King of Israel!" **8.** And one of them brought a crown of thorns and put it on the Lord's head. **9.** And others who stood by spat on his face, and others buffeted him on the cheeks, others nudged him with a reed, and some scourged him, saying, "With such honour let us honour the Son of God."

4:10. And they brought two malefactors and crucified the Lord in the midst between them. But he held his peace, as if he felt no pain. **11.** And when they had set up the cross, they wrote upon it: this is the King of Israel. **12.** And they laid down his garments before him and divided them among themselves and cast the lot upon them. **13.** But one of the malefactors rebuked them, saying, "We have landed in suffering for the deed of wickedness which we have committed, but this man, who has become the saviour of men, what wrong has he done you?" **14.** And they were wroth with him and commanded that his legs should not be broken, so that he might die in torments.

5:15. Now it was midday and a darkness covered all Judaea. And they became anxious and uneasy lest the sun had already set, since he was still alive. [For] it stands written for them: the sun should not set on one that has been put to death. 16. And one of them said, "Give him to drink gall with vinegar." And they mixed it and gave him to drink. 17. And they fulfilled all things and completed the measure of their sins on their head. 18. And many went about with lamps, [and] as they supposed that it was night, they went to bed (or: they stumbled). 19. And the Lord called out and cried: "My power, O power, thou hast forsaken me!" And having said this he was taken up. 20. And at the same hour the veil of the temple in Jerusalem was rent in two.

6:21. And then the Jews drew nails from the hands of the Lord and laid him on the earth. And the whole earth shook and there came a great fear. 22. Then the sun shone [again], and it was found to be the ninth hour. 23. And the Jews rejoiced and gave his body to Joseph that he might bury it, since he had seen all the good that he (Jesus) had done. 24. And he took the Lord, washed him, wrapped him in linen and brought him into his own sepulchre, called Joseph's Garden.

7:25. Then the Jews and the elders and the priests, perceiving what great evil they had done to themselves, began to lament and to say, "Woe on our sins, the judgment and the end of Jerusalem is drawn nigh." 26. But I mourned with my fellows, and being wounded in heart we hid ourselves, for we were sought after by them as evildoers and as persons who wanted to set fire to the temple. 27. Because of all these things we were fasting and sat mourning and weeping night and day until the Sabbath.

8:28. But the scribes and Pharisees and elders, being assembled together and hearing that all the people were murmuring and beating their breasts, saying, "If at his death these exceeding great signs have come to pass, behold, how righteous he was!" 29. They were afraid and came to Pilate, entreating him and saying, 30. "Give us soldiers that we may watch his sepulchre for three days, lest his disciples come and steal him away and the people suppose that he is risen from the dead, and do us harm." 31. And Pilate gave them Petronius the centurion with soldiers to watch the sepulchre. And with them there came elders and scribes to the sepulchre. 32. And all who were there, together with the centurion and the soldiers, rolled thither a great stone and laid it against the entrance to the sepulchre 33. and put on it seven seals, pitched a tent and kept watch. 9:34. Early in the morning, when the Sabbath dawned, there came a crowd from Jerusalem and the country round about to see the sepulchre that had been sealed.

35. Now in the night in which the Lord's day dawned, when the soldiers, two by two in every watch, were keeping guard, there rang out a loud noise in

heaven, 36. and they saw the heavens opened and two men come down from there in a great brightness and draw nigh to the sepulchre. 37. That stone which had been laid against the entrance to the sepulchre started of itself to roll and gave way to the side, and the sepulchre was opened, and both the young men entered. 10:38. When now those soldiers saw this, they awakened the centurion and the elders—for they also were there to assist at the watch. 39. And whilst they were relating what they had seen, they saw again three men come out from the sepulchre, and two of them sustaining the other, and a cross following them, 40. and the heads of the two reaching to heaven, but that of him who was led of them by the hand overpassing the heavens. 41. And they heard a voice out of the heavens crying, "Thou hast preached to them that sleep," 42. and from the cross there was heard the answer, "Yea." 11:43. Those men therefore took counsel with one another to go and report this to Pilate. 44. And whilst they were still deliberating, the heavens were again seen to open, and a man descended and entered into the sepulchre. 45. When those who were of the centurion's company saw this they hastened by night to Pilate, abandoning the sepulchre which they were guarding, and reported everything that they had seen, being full of disquietude and saying, "In truth he was the Son of God." 46. Pilate answered and said, "I am clean from the blood of the Son of God, upon such a thing have you decided." 47. Then all came to him, beseeching him and urgently calling upon him to command the centurion and the soldiers to tell no one what they had seen. 48. "For it is better for us," they said, "to make ourselves guilty of the greatest sin before God than to fall into the hands of the people of the Jews and be stoned." 49. Pilate therefore commanded the centurion and the soldiers to say nothing.

12:50. Early in the morning of the Lord's day Mary Magdalene, a woman disciple of the Lord—for fear of the Jews, since (they) were inflamed with wrath, she had not done at the sepulchre of the Lord what women are wont to do for those beloved of them who die—took 51. with her her woman friends and came to the sepulchre where he was laid. 52. And they feared lest the Jews see them, and said, "Although we could not weep and lament on that day when he was crucified, yet let us now do so at his sepulchre. 53. But who will roll away for us the stone also that is set on the entrance to the sepulchre, that we may go in and sit beside him and do what is due?— 54. For the stone was great,—and we fear lest any one see us. And if we cannot do so, let us at least put down at the entrance what we bring for a memorial of him and let us weep and lament until we have again gone home." 13:55. So they went and found the sepulchre opened. And they came near, stooped down and saw there a young man sitting in the midst of the sepulchre, comely and

clothed with a brightly shining robe, who said to them, 56. "Wherefore are ye
come? Whom seek ye? Not him that was crucified? He is risen and gone. But
if ye believe not, stoop this way and see the place where he lay, for he is not
here. For he is risen and is gone thither whence he was sent." 57. Then the
women fled affrighted.

14:58. Now it was the last day of unleavened bread and many went away
and repaired to their homes, since the feast was at an end. 59. But we, the
twelve disciples of the Lord, wept and mourned, and each one, very grieved
for what had come to pass, went to his own home. 60. But I, Simon Peter,
and my brother Andrew took our nets and went to the sea.

The Book of James

The stories of the birth of Jesus are secondary additions to the Gospels
of Matthew and Luke. Mark, by most reckonings the earliest gospel,
seems never to have possessed such a story, and begins with the legend
of the adoption of Jesus to divine sonship at the time of his baptism
(Mark 1:9-11). Theologically, the birth legends in the other Synoptic
Gospels serve to correct the view of Mark's Gospel by dating Jesus'
sonship from the time of his conception, making him a god by
nature rather than by adoption. The Gospel of John presents an
altogether different view describing Jesus as the eternal word (logos) of
God, that is, an integral, timeless, and continuing *aspect* of God made
manifest in the person of Jesus Christ (John 1:1-5). While it is seldom
commented on by theologians and ministers, the Fourth Gospel
completely contradicts the synoptic stories of the human birth of Jesus
(John 1:13-14).

All this goes to show that there is no harmony among the Gospel
accounts of the origin of Jesus. Each Gospel presents its own theological message and reflects disagreements that later blossom into the
great christological battles of the third and fourth centuries. At the end
of these struggles, a version of the logos-christology of the Fourth
Gospel was given formal preference and definition by the vote of
church councils meeting at Nicaea in 325 and at Constantinople in
381: Jesus was proclaimed to be "God from God, light from light, true
God of true God, begotten but not created, and of one substance with

the father." By contrast, the adoptionist christology of the oldest gospel
survived only among heretical groups like the Ebionites, a group of
Jewish Christians who remained outside the mainstream of church
development.

The following apocryphal gospels are concerned with the human
side of the birth of Jesus, though they are both legendary in character.
The Book of James dates from the second century and survives in its
original Greek form and in several Near Eastern versions. The opening
section concerning the nativity and childhood of the virgin gained
prominence from the early Middle Ages onward among adherents of
the cult of Mary.

Book of James, or Protevangelium

I. 1 In the histories of the twelve tribes of Israel *it is written that* there was
one Ioacim, exceeding rich: and he offered his gifts twofold, saying: That
which is of my superfluity shall be for the whole people, and that which is for
my forgiveness shall be for the Lord, for a propitiation unto me.

2 Now the great day of the Lord drew nigh and the children of Israel
offered their gifts. And Reuben stood over against him saying: It is not
lawful for thee to offer thy gifts first, for thou has gotten no seed in Israel. 3
And Ioacim was sore grieved, and went unto *the record of* the twelve tribes of
the people, saying: I will look upon *the record of* the twelve tribes of Israel, whether I only have not gotten seed in Israel. And he searched, and
found *concerning* all the righteous that they had raised up seed in Israel. And
he remembered the patriarch Abraham, how in the last days God gave him
a son, even Isaac. 4 And Ioacim was sore grieved, and showed not himself
to his wife, but betook himself into the wilderness, and pitched his tent there,
and fasted forty days and forty nights, saying within himself: I will not go
down either for meat or for drink until the Lord my God visit me, and my
prayer shall be unto me meat and drink.

II. 1 Now his wife Anna lamented with two lamentations, and bewailed
herself with two bewailings, saying: I will bewail my widowhood, and I will
bewail my childlessness.

2 And the great day of the Lord drew nigh, and Judith her handmaid said
unto her: How long humblest thou thy soul? The great day of the Lord hath
come, and it is not lawful for thee to mourn: but take this headband, which
the mistress of *my* work gave me, and it is not lawful for me to put it on,

forasmuch as I am an handmaid, and it hath a mark of royalty. And Anna said: Get thee from me. Lo! I have done nothing (*or* I will not do so) and the Lord hath greatly humbled me: peradventure one gave it to thee in subtilty, and thou art come to make me partaker in thy sin. And Judith said: How shall I curse thee, seeing the Lord hath shut up thy womb, to give thee no fruit in Israel?

3 And Anna was sore grieved [and mourned with a great mourning because she was reproached by all the tribes of Israel. And coming to herself she said: What shall I do? I will pray with weeping unto the Lord my God that he visit me]. And she put off her mourning garments and cleansed (*or* adorned) her head and put on her bridal garments: and about the ninth hour she went down into the garden to walk there. And she saw a laurel-tree and sat down underneath it and besought the Lord saying: O God of our fathers, bless me, and hearken unto my prayer, as thou didst bless the womb of Sarah, and gavest her a son, even Isaac.

III. 1 And looking up to the heaven she espied a nest of sparrows in the laurel-tree, and made a lamentation within herself, saying: Woe unto me, who begat me? And what womb brought me forth, for I am become a curse before the children of Israel, and I am reproached, and they have mocked me forth out of the temple of the Lord? 2 Woe unto me, unto what am I likened? I am not likened unto the fowls of the heaven, for even the fowls of the heaven are fruitful before thee, O Lord. Woe unto me, unto what am I likened? I am not likened unto the beasts of the earth, for even the beasts of the earth are fruitful before thee, O Lord. Woe unto me, unto what am I likened? I am not likened unto these waters, for even these waters are fruited before thee, O Lord. 3 Woe unto me, unto what am I likened? I am not likened unto this earth, for even this earth bringeth forth her fruits in due season and blesseth thee, O Lord.

IV. 1 And behold an angel of the Lord appeared, saying unto her: Anna, Anna, the Lord hath hearkened unto thy prayer, and thou shalt conceive and bear, and thy seed shall be spoken of in the whole world. And Anna said: As the Lord my God liveth, if I bring forth either male or female, I will bring it for a gift unto the Lord My God, and it shall be ministering unto him all the days of its life.

2 And behold there came two messengers saying unto her: Behold Ioacim thy husband cometh with his flocks: for an angel of the Lord came down unto him saying: Ioacim, Ioacim, the Lord God hath hearkened unto thy prayer. Get thee down hence, for behold thy wife Anna hath conceived. 3 And Ioacim gat him down and called his herdsmen saying: Bring me hither ten lambs

without blemish and without spot, and they shall be for the Lord my God; and bring me twelve tender calves, and they shall be for the priests and for the assembly of the elders; and a hundred kids for the whole people.

4 And behold Ioacim came with his flocks, and Anna stood at the gate and saw Ioacim coming, and ran and hung upon his neck, saying: Now know I that the Lord God hath greatly blessed me: for behold the widow is no more a widow, and she that was childless shall conceive. And Ioacim rested the first day in his house.

V. 1 And on the morrow, he offered his gifts, saying in himself: If the Lord God be reconciled unto me, the plate *that is upon the forehead* of the priest will make it manifest unto me. And Ioacim offered his gifts and looked earnestly upon the plate of the priest when he went up unto the altar of the Lord, and he saw no sin in himself. And Ioacim said: Now know I that the Lord is become propitious unto me and hath forgiven all my sins. And he went down from the temple of the Lord justified, and went unto his house.

2 And her months were fulfilled, and in the ninth month Anna brought forth. And she said unto the midwife: What have I brought forth? And she said: A female. And Anna said: My soul is magnified this day, and she laid herself down. And when the days were fulfilled, Anna purified herself and gave suck to the child and called her name Mary.

VI. 1 And day by day the child waxed strong, and when she was six months old her mother stood her upon the ground to try if she would stand; and she walked seven steps and returned unto her bosom. And she caught her up, saying: As the Lord my God liveth, thou shalt walk no more upon this ground, until I bring thee into the temple of the Lord. And she made a sanctuary in her bedchamber and suffered nothing common or unclean to pass through it. And she called for the daughters of the Hebrews that were undefiled, and they carried her hither and thither.

2 And the first year of the child was *fulfilled,* and Ioacim made a great feast and bade the priests and the scribes and the assembly of the elders and the whole people of Israel. And Ioacim brought the child to the priests, and they blessed her, saying: O God of our fathers, bless this child and give her a name renowned for ever among all generations. And all the people said: So be it, so be it. Amen. And he brought her to the high priests, and they blessed her, saying: O God of the high places, look upon this child, and bless her with the last blessing which hath no successor.

3 And her mother caught her up into the sanctuary of her bedchamber and gave her suck.

And Anna made a song unto the Lord God, saying:

I will sing an hymn unto the Lord my God, because he hath visited me and taken away from me the reproach of mine enemies, and the Lord hath given me a fruit of his righteousness, single *and* manifold before him. Who shall declare unto the sons of Reuben that Anna giveth suck? Hearken, hearken, ye twelve tribes of Israel, that Anna giveth suck. And she laid the child to rest in the bedchamber of her sanctuary, and went forth and ministered unto them. And when the feast was ended, they gat them down rejoicing, and glorifying the God of Israel.

VII. 1 And unto the child her months were added: and the child became two years old. And Ioacim said: Let us bring her up to the temple of the Lord that we may pay the promise which we promised; lest the Lord require it of us (*lit.* send unto us), and our gift become unacceptable. And Anna said: Let us wait until the third year, that the child may not long after her father or mother. And Ioacim said: Let us wait.

2 And the child became three years old, and Ioacim said: Call for the daughters of the Hebrews that are undefiled, and let them take every one a lamp, and let them be burning, that the child turn not backward and her heart be taken captive away from the temple of the Lord. And they did so until they were gone up into the temple of the Lord.

And the priest received her and kissed her and blessed her and said: The Lord hath magnified thy name among all generations: in thee in the latter days shall the Lord make manifest his redemption unto the children of Israel. And he made her to sit upon the third step of the altar. And the Lord put grace upon her and she danced with her feet and all the house of Israel loved her.

VIII. 1 And her parents gat them down marvelling, and praising the Lord God because the child was not turned away backward.

And Mary was in the temple of the Lord as a dove that is nurtured; and she received food from the hand of an angel.

2 And when she was twelve years old, there was a council of the priests, saying: Behold Mary is become twelve years old in the temple of the Lord. What then shall we do with her? lest she pollute the sanctuary of the Lord. And they said unto the high priest: Thou standest over the altar of the Lord. Enter in and pray concerning her: And whatsoever the Lord shall reveal to thee, that let us do.

3 And the high priest took the vestment with the twelve belts and went in unto the Holy of Holies and prayed concerning her. And lo, an angel of the Lord appeared saying unto him: Zacharias, Zacharias, go forth and assemble them that are widowers of the people, and let them bring every man a rod,

and to whomsoever the Lord shall show a sign, his wife shall she be. And the heralds went forth over all the country round about Judaea, and the trumpet of the Lord sounded, and all men ran thereto.

IX. 1 And Joseph cast down his adze and ran to meet them, and when they were gathered together they went to the high priest and took their rods *with them*. And he took the rods of them all and went into the temple and prayed. And when he had finished the prayer he took the rods and went forth and gave them back to them: and there was no sign upon them. But Joseph received the last rod: and lo, a dove came forth of the rod and flew upon the head of Joseph. And the priest said unto Joseph: Unto thee hath it fallen to take the virgin of the Lord and keep her for thyself. 2 And Joseph refused, saying, I have sons, and I am an old man, but she is a girl: lest I become a laughing-stock to the children of Israel. And the priest said unto Joseph: Fear the Lord thy God, and remember what things God did unto Dathan and Abiram and Korah, how the earth clave and they were swallowed up because of their gainsaying. And now fear thou, Joseph, lest it be so in thine house. And Joseph was afraid, and took her to keep her for himself. And Joseph said unto Mary: Lo, I have received thee out of the temple of the Lord: and now do I leave thee in my house, and I go away to build my buildings and I will come *again* unto thee. The Lord shall watch over thee.

X. 1 Now there was a council of the priests, and they said: Let us make a veil for the temple of the Lord. And the priest said: Call unto me pure virgins of the tribe of David. And the officers departed and sought and found seven virgins. And the priests called to mind the child Mary, that she was of the tribe of David and was undefiled before God: and the officers went and fetched her. And they brought them into the temple of the Lord, and the priest said: Cast me lots, which *of you* shall weave the gold and the undefiled (the white) and the fine linen and the silk and the hyacinthine, and the scarlet and the true purple. And the lot of the true purple and the scarlet fell unto Mary, and she took them and went unto her house.

[And at that season Zacharias became dumb, and Samuel was in his stead until the time when Zacharias spake *again*.].

But Mary took the scarlet and began to spin it.

XI. 1 And she took the pitcher and went forth to fill it with water; and lo a voice saying: Hail, thou that art highly favoured; the Lord is with thee: blessed art thou among women.

And she looked about her upon the right hand and upon the left, to see whence this voice should be: and being filled with trembling she went to her house and set down the pitcher, and took the purple and sat down upon her seat and drew out the thread.

2 And behold an angel of the Lord stood before her saying: Fear not, Mary, for thou hast found grace before the Lord of all things, and thou shalt conceive of his word. And she, when she heard it, questioned in herself, saying: Shall I *verily* conceive of the living God, and bring forth after the manner of all women? And the angel of the Lord said: Not so, Mary, for a power of the Lord shall overshadow thee: wherefore also that holy thing which shall be born of thee shall be called the Son of the Highest. And thou shalt call his name Jesus: for he shall save his people from their sins. And Mary said: Behold the handmaid of the Lord is before him: be it unto me according to thy word.

XII. 1 And she made the purple and the scarlet and brought them unto the priest. And the priest blessed her and said: Mary, the Lord God hath magnified thy name, and thou shalt be blessed among all generations of the earth. 2 And Mary rejoiced and went away unto Elizabeth her kinswoman: and she knocked at the door. And Elizabeth when she heard it cast down the scarlet (*al.* the wool) and ran to the door and opened it, and when she saw Mary she blessed her and said: Whence is this to me that the mother of my Lord shall come unto me? for behold that which is in me leaped and blessed thee. And Mary forgat the mysteries which Gabriel the archangel had told her, and she looked up unto the heaven and said: Who am I, Lord, that all the generations of the earth do bless me? 3 And she abode three months with Elizabeth, and day by day her womb grew: and Mary was afraid and departed unto her house and hid herself from the children of Israel. Now she was sixteen years old when these mysteries came to pass.

XIII. 1 Now it was the sixth month with her, and behold Joseph came from his building, and he entered into his house and found her great with child. And he smote his face, and cast himself down upon the ground on sackcloth and wept bitterly, saying: With what countenance shall I look unto the Lord my God? and what prayer shall I make concerning this maiden? for I received her out of the temple of the Lord My God a virgin, and have not kept her safe. Who is he that hath ensnared me? Who hath done this evil in mine house and hath defiled the virgin? Is not the story of Adam repeated in me? for as at the hour of his giving thanks the serpent came and found Eve alone and deceived her, so hath it befallen me also. 2 And Joseph arose from off the sackcloth and called Mary and said unto her: O thou that wast cared for by God, why hast thou done this? thou hast forgotten the Lord thy God. Why hast thou humbled thy soul, thou that wast nourished up in the Holy of Holies and didst receive food at the hand of an angel? 3 But she wept bitterly, saying: "I am pure and I know not a man. And Joseph said unto her: Whence then is that which is in thy womb? and she said: As the Lord my God liveth, I know not whence it is come unto me.

XIV. 1 And Joseph was sore afraid and ceased from *speaking unto* her (*or* left her alone), and pondered what he should do with her. And Joseph said: If I hide her sin, I shall be found fighting against the law of the Lord: and if I manifest her unto the children of Israel, I fear lest that which is in her to be the seed of the judgement of death. What then shall I do? I will let her go from me privily. And the night came upon him. 2 And behold an angel of the Lord appeared unto him in a dream, saying: Fear not this child, for that which is in her is of the Holy Ghost, and she shall bear a son and thou shalt call his name Jesus, for he shall save his people from their sins. And Joseph arose from sleep and glorified the God of Israel which had shown this favour upon her: and he watched over her.

XV. 1 Now Annas the scribe came unto him and said to him: Wherefore didst thou not appear in our assembly? and Joseph said unto him: I was weary with the journey, and I rested the first day. And *Annas* turned him about and saw Mary great with child. 2 And he went hastily to the priest and said unto him: Joseph, to whom thou bearest witness [that he is righteous] hath sinned grievously. And the priest said: Wherein? And he said: The virgin whom he received out of the temple of the Lord, he hath defiled her, and married her by stealth (*lit.* stolen her marriage), and hath not declared it to the children of Israel. And the priest answered and said: Hath Joseph done this? And Annas the scribe said: Send officers, and thou shalt find the virgin great with child. And the officers went and found as he had said, and they brought her together with Joseph unto the place of judgement. 3 And the priest said: Mary, wherefore hast thou done this, and wherefore hast thou humbled thy soul and forgotten the Lord thy God, thou that wast nurtured in the Holy of Holies and didst receive food at the hand of an angel and didst hear *the* hymns and didst dance before *the Lord,* wherefore hast thou done this?

But she wept bitterly, saying: As the Lord my God liveth I am pure before him and I know not a man. 4 And the priest said unto Joseph: Wherefore hast thou done this? And Joseph said: As the Lord my God liveth I am pure as concerning her. And the priest said: Bear no false witness but speak the truth: thou hast married her by stealth and hast not declared it unto the children of Israel, and hast not bowed thine head under the mighty hand that thy seed should be blessed. And Joseph held his peace.

XVI. 1 And the priest said: Restore the virgin whom thou didst receive out of the temple of the Lord. And Joseph was full of weeping. And the priest said: I will give you to drink of the water of the conviction of the Lord, and it will make manifest your sins before your eyes. 2 And the priest took thereof and made Joseph drink and sent him into the hill-country. And he returned whole. He made Mary also drink and sent her into the hill-country. And she returned whole. And all the people marvelled, because sin appeared not in them. 3 And the priest said: If the Lord God hath not made your sin manifest, neither do I condemn you. And he let them go. And Joseph took Mary and departed unto his house rejoicing, and glorifying the God of Israel.

XVII. 1 Now there went out a decree from Augustus the king that all that were in Bethlehem of Judea should be recorded. And Joseph said: I will record my sons: but this child, what shall I do with her? how shall I record her? as my wife? *nay*, I am ashamed. Or as my daughter? but all the children of Israel know that she is not my daughter. This day of the Lord shall do as the Lord willeth. 2 And he saddled the she-ass, and set her upon it, and his son led it and Joseph followed after. And they drew near (unto Bethlehem) within three miles: and Joseph turned himself about and saw her of a sad countenance and said within himself: Peradventure that which is within her paineth her. And again Joseph turned himself about and saw her laughing, and said unto her: Mary, what aileth thee that I see thy face at one time laughing and at another time sad? And Mary said unto Joseph: It is because I behold two peoples with mine eyes, the one weeping and lamenting and the other rejoicing and exulting.

3 And they came to the midst of the way, and Mary said unto him: Take me down from the ass, for that which is within me presseth me, to come forth. And he took her down from the ass and said unto her: Whither shall I take thee to hide thy shame? for the place is desert.

XVIII. 1 And he found a cave there and brought her into it, and set his sons by her: and he went forth and sought for a midwife of the Hebrews in the country of Bethlehem.

2 Now I Joseph was walking, and I walked not. And I looked up to the air and saw the air in amazement. And I looked up unto the pole of the heaven and saw it standing still, and the fowls of the heaven without motion. And I looked upon the earth and saw a dish set, and workmen lying *by it,* and their hands were in the dish: and they that were chewing chewed not, and they that were lifting *the food* lifted it not, and they that put it to their mouth put it not thereto, but the faces of all of them were looking upward. And behold there were sheep being driven, and they went not forward but stood still; and the shepherd lifted his hand to smite them with his staff, and his hand remained up. And I looked upon the stream of the river and saw

the mouths of the kids upon *the water* and they drank not. And of a sudden all things moved onward in their course.

XIX. 1 And behold a woman coming down from the hill-country, and she said to me: Man, whither goest thou? And I said: I seek a midwife of the Hebrews. And she answered and said unto me: Art thou of Israel? And I said unto her: Yea. And she said: And who is she that bringeth forth in the cave? And I said: She that is betrothed unto me. And she said to me: Is she not thy wife? And I said to her: It is Mary that was nurtured up in the temple of the Lord: and I received her to wife by lot: and she is not my wife, but she hath conception by the Holy Ghost.

And the midwife said unto him: Is this the truth? And Joseph said unto her: Come hither and see. And the midwife went with him.

2 And they stood in the place of the cave: and behold a bright cloud overshadowing the cave. And the midwife said: My soul is magnified this day, because mine eyes have seen marvellous things: for salvation is born unto Israel. And immediately the cloud withdrew itself out of the cave, and a great light appeared in the cave so that our eyes could not endure it. And by little and little that light withdrew itself until the young child appeared: and it went and took the breast of its mother Mary.

And the midwife cried aloud and said: Great unto me today is this day, in that I have seen this new sight. 3 And the midwife went forth of the cave and Salome met her. And she said to her: Salome, Salome, a new sight have I to tell thee. A virgin hath brought forth, which her nature alloweth not. And Salome said: As the Lord my God liveth, if I make not trial and prove her nature I will not believe that a virgin hath brought forth.

XX. 1 And the midwife went in and said unto Mary: Order thyself, for *there is no small contention* arisen concerning thee. And Salome made trial and cried out and said: Woe unto mine iniquity and mine unbelief, because I have tempted the living God, and lo, my hand falleth away from me in fire. And she bowed her knees unto the Lord, saying: O God of my fathers, remember that I am the seed of Abraham and Isaac and Jacob: make me not a public example unto the children of Israel, but restore me unto the poor, for thou knowest, Lord, that in thy name did I perform my cures, and did receive my hire of thee. 3 And lo, an angel of the Lord appeared, saying unto her: Salome, Salome, the Lord hath hearkened to thee: bring thine hand near unto the young child and take him up, and there shall be unto thee salvation and joy. 4 And Salome came near and took him up, saying: I will do him worship, for a great king is born unto Israel. And behold immediately Salome was healed: and she went forth of the cave justified. And lo, a voice saying:

Salome, Salome, tell none of the marvels which thou hast seen, until the child enter into Jerusalem.

XXI. 1 And behold, Joseph made him ready to go forth into Judea. And there came a great tumult in Bethlehem of Judea; for there came wise men, saying: Where is he that is born king of the Jews? for we have seen his star in the east and are come to worship him. 2 and when Herod heard it he was troubled and sent officers unto the wise men. And he sent for the high priests and examined them, saying: How is it written concerning the Christ, where he is born? They say unto him: In Bethlehem of Judea: for so it is written. And he let them go. And he examined the wise men, saying unto them: What sign saw ye concerning the king that is born? And the wise men said: We saw a very great star shining among those stars and dimming them so that the stars appeared not: and thereby knew we that a king was born unto Israel, and we came to worship him. And Herod said: Go and seek for him, and if ye find him, tell me, that I also may come and worship him. 3 And the wise men went forth. And lo, the star which they saw in the east went before them until they entered into the cave: and it stood over the head of the cave. And the wise men saw the young child with Mary his mother: and they brought out of their scrip gifts, gold and frankincense and myrrh. 4 And being warned by the angel that they should not enter into Judea, they went into their own country by another way.

XXII. 1 But when Herod perceived that he was mocked by the wise men, he was wroth, and sent murderers, saying unto them: Slay the children from two years old and under. 2 And when Mary heard that the children were being slain, she was afraid, and took the young child and wrapped him in swaddling clothes and laid him in an ox-manger.

3 But Elizabeth when she heard that they sought for John, took him and went up into the hill-country and looked about her where she should hide him: and there was no hiding-place. And Elizabeth groaned and said with a loud voice: O mountain of God, receive thou a mother with a child. For Elizabeth was not able to go up. And immediately the mountain clave asunder and took her in. And there was a light shining *alway* for them: for an angel of the Lord was with them, keeping watch over them.

XXIII. 1 Now Herod sought for John, and sent officers to Zacharias, saying: Where hast thou hidden thy son? And he answered and said unto them: I am a minister of God and attend continually upon the temple of the Lord: I know not where my son is. 2 And the officers departed and told Herod all these things. And Herod was wroth and said: His son is to be king over Israel. And he sent unto him again saying: Say the truth: where is thy son? for thou knowest that thy blood is under my hand. And the officers departed and told him all these things. 3 And Zacharias said: I am a martyr of God if thou sheddest my blood: for my spirit the Lord shall receive, because thou sheddest innocent blood in the fore-court of the temple of the Lord.

And about the dawning of the day Zacharias was slain. And the children of Israel knew not that he was slain.

XXIV. 1 But the priests entered in at the hour of the salutation, and the blessing of Zacharias met them not according to the manner. And the priests stood waiting for Zacharias, to salute him with the prayer, and to glorify the Most High. 2 But as he delayed to come, they were all afraid: and one of them took courage and entered in: and he saw beside the altar congealed blood: and a voice saying: Zacharias hath been slain, and his blood shall not be wiped out until his avenger come. And when he heard that word he was afraid, and went forth and told the priests. 3 And they took courage and went in and saw that which was done: and the panels of the temple did wail: and they rent [*al.* and *(the panels)* were split, etc. See Amos viii. 3 (lxx)] *their clothes* from the top to the bottom. And his body they found not, but his blood they found turned into stone. And they feared, and went forth and told all the people that Zacharias was slain. And all the tribes of the people heard it, and they mourned for him and lamented him three days and three nights. And after the three days the priests took counsel whom they should set in his stead: and the lot came up upon Symeon. Now he it was which was warned by the Holy Ghost that he should not see death until he should see the Christ in the flesh.

XXV. 1 Now I, James, which wrote this story in Jerusalem, when there arose a tumult when Herod died, withdrew myself into the wilderness until the tumult ceased in Jerusalem.

Glorifying the Lord God which gave me the gift, and the wisdom to write this history.

2 And grace shall be with those that fear our Lord Jesus Christ: to whom be glory for ever and ever. Amen.

The Infancy Gospel of Thomas

This gospel, purported to come from the hand of Thomas the Apostle, dates from the third century, though the earliest complete version comes in a Syriac manuscript of the sixth century. those who come to this work for the first time are often struck by its portrayal of the young Jesus as a callous wonder-worker who delights in reckless demonstrations of power. In fact, such stories must have circulated widely even in the first century: Luke incorporates an apparently diluted version of such an anecdote in his Gospel (2:41-51), and the story of the changing of water into wine at Cana (John 2:1-11) looks suspiciously like a modified infancy story. The *Tol'doth Jeshu* (pp. 50-53) also preserves the tradition of the infant Jesus' unruliness. These examples notwithstanding, the childhood of Jesus finds no place in any of the New Testament Gospels, a fact which may in itself suggest editorial discretion on the part of the New Testament writers. The text used here is a slightly modernized version of M. R. James's translation in *The Apocryphal New Testament*.

GREEK TEXT A

I. 1. Thomas the Israelite, tell unto you, even all the brethren that are of the Gentiles, to make known unto you the works of the childhood of our Lord Jesus Christ and his mighty deeds, even all that he did when he was born in our land: whereof the beginning is thus:

II. 1 This little child Jesus when he was five years old was playing at the ford of a brook: and he gathered together the waters that flowed *there* into pools, and made them straightway clean, and commanded them by his word alone. 2 And having made soft clay, he fashioned thereof twelve sparrows. And it was the sabbath when he did these things (*or* made them). And there were also many other little children playing with him.

3 And a certain Jew when he saw what Jesus did, playing upon the sabbath day, departed straightway and told his father Joseph: Lo, thy child is at the brook, and he hath taken clay and fashioned twelve little birds, and hath polluted the sabbath day. 4 And Joseph came to the place and saw: and cried out to him, saying: Wherefore doest thou these things on the sabbath, which it is not lawful to do? But Jesus clapped his hands together and cried out to the sparrows and said to them: Go! and the sparrows took their flight and went away chirping. 5 And when the Jews saw it they were amazed, and departed and told their chief men that which they had seen Jesus do.

III. 1 But the son of Annas the scribe was standing there with Joseph; and he took a branch of a willow and dispersed the waters which Jesus had gathered together. 2 And when Jesus saw what was done, he was wroth and said unto him: O evil, ungodly, and foolish one, what hurt did the pools and the waters do thee? behold, now also thou shalt be withered like a tree, and shalt not bear leaves, neither root, nor fruit. 3 And straightway that lad withered up wholly, but Jesus departed and went unto Joseph's house. But the parents of him that was withered took him up, bewailing his youth, and brought him to Joseph, and accused him "for thou that hast such a child which doeth such deeds."

IV. 1 After that again he went through the village, and a child ran and dashed against his shoulder. And Jesus was provoked and said unto him: Thou shall not finish thy course (*lit.* go all thy way). And immediately he fell down and died. But certain [people] when they saw what was done said: Whence was this young child born, for that every word of his is an accomplished work? And the parents of him that was dead came unto Joseph, and blamed him, saying: Thou that hast such a child canst not dwell with us in the village: or do thou teach him to bless and not to curse: for he slayeth our children.

V. 1 And Joseph called the young child apart and admonished him, saying: Wherefore doest thou such things, that these suffer and hate us and persecute us? But Jesus said: I know that these thy words are not thine: nevertheless for thy sake I will hold my peace: but they shall bear their punishment. And straightaway they that accused him were smitten with blindness. 2 And they that saw it were sore afraid and perplexed, and said concerning him that every word which he spake, whether it were good or bad, was a deed, and became a marvel. And when they (he?) saw that Jesus had so done, Joseph arose and took him upon his ear and wrung it sore. 3 And the young child was wroth and said unto him: It sufficeth thee (*or* them) to seek and not to find, and verily thou hast done unwisely: knowest thou not that I am thine? vex me not.

VI. 1 Now a certain teacher, Zacchaeus by name, stood there, and he heard in part when Jesus said these things to his father, and he marvelled greatly that being a young child he spake such matters. 2 And after a few days he came near unto Joseph and said unto him: Thou hast a wise child, and he hath understanding. Come, deliver him to me that he may learn letters. And I will teach him with the letters all knowledge, and that he salute all the elders and honor them as grandfathers and fathers, and love them of his own years. 3 And he told him all the letters from Alpha to Omega clearly, with much questioning. But *Jesus* looked upon Zacchaeus the teacher and saith unto him: Thou that knowest not the Alpha according to its nature, how canst thou teach others the Beta? thou hypocrite first, if thou knowest it, teach the Alpha, and then will we believe thee concerning the Beta. Then began he to confound the mouth of the teacher concerning the first letter, and he could not prevail to answer him. 4 And in the hearing of many the young child said to Zacchaeus: Hear, O teacher, the ordinance of the first letter and pay heed to this, how that it hath [*what follows is really unintelligible in this and in all the parallel texts: a literal version would run somewhat thus:* how that it hath lines, and a middle mark, which thou seest, common to both, going apart; coming together, raised up on high, dancing *(a corrupt word)*, of three signs, like in kind *(a corrupt word)*, balanced, equal in measure]: thou hast the rules of the Alpha.

VII. 1 Now when Zacchaeus the teacher heard such and so many allegories of the first letter spoken by the young child, he was perplexed at his answer and his instruction being so great, and said to them that were there: Woe is me, wretch that I am, I am confounded: I have brought shame to myself by drawing to me this young child. 2 Take him away, therefore, I beseech thee, my brother Joseph: I cannot endure the severity of his look, I cannot once make clear my (*or* his) word. This young child is not earthly born: this is one that can tame even fire: belike this is one begotten before the making of the world. What belly bare this, what womb nurtured it? I know not. Woe is me, O my friend, he putteth me from my sense, I cannot follow his understanding. I have deceived myself, thrice wretched man that I am: I strove to get me a disciple and I am found to have a master. 3 I think, O my friends, upon my shame, for that being old I have been overcome by a young child; and I am even ready to faint and die because of the boy, for I am not able at this present hour to look him in the face. And when all men say that I have been overcome by a little child, what have I to say? and what can I tell concerning the lines of the first letter whereof he spake to me? I am ignorant, O my friends, for neither beginning or end of it (*or* him) do I know. 4 Wherefore I beseech thee, my brother Joseph, take him away unto thine house: for he is somewhat great, whether god or angel or what I should call him, I know not.

VIII. 1 And as the Jews were counseling Zacchaeus, the young child laughed greatly and said: Now let those bear fruit that were barren (*Gr.* that are thine) and let them see that were blind in heart. I am come from above that I may curse them, and call them to the things that are above, even as he commanded which hath sent me for your sakes. 2 And when the young child ceased speaking, immediately all they were made whole which had come under his curse. And no man after that durst provoke him, lest he should curse him, and he should be maimed.

IX. 1 Now after certain days Jesus was playing in the upper story of a certain house, and one of the young children that played with him fell down from the house and died. And the other children when they saw it fled, and Jesus remained alone. 2 And the parents of him that was dead came and accused him that he had cast him down. (And Jesus said: I did not cast him down) but they reviled him still. 3 Then Jesus leaped down from the roof and stood by the body of the child and cried with a loud voice and said: Zeno (for so was his name called), arise and tell me, did I cast thee down? And straightway he arose and said: Nay, Lord, thou didst not cast me down, but didst raise me up. And when they saw it they were amazed: and the parents of the child glorified God for the sign which had come to pass, and worshipped Jesus.

X. 1 After a few days, a certain young man was cleaving wood in the neighborhood (*MSS.* corner), and the axe fell and cut in sunder the sole of his foot, and losing much blood he was at the point to die. 2 And when there was a tumult and concourse, the young child Jesus also ran thither, and by force passed through the multitude, and took hold upon the foot of the young man that was smitten, and straightway it was healed. And he said unto the young man: Arise now and cleave the wood, and remember me. But when the multitude saw what was done they worshipped the young child, saying: Verily the spirit of God dwelleth in this young child.

XI. 1 Now when he was six years old, his mother sendeth him to draw water and bear it into the house, and gave him a pitcher: but in the press he struck *against another* and the pitcher was broken. 2 But Jesus spread out the garment which was upon him and filled it with water and brought it to his mother. And when his mother saw what was done she kissed him; and she kept within herself the mysteries which she saw him do.

XII. 1 Again, in the time of sowing the young child went forth with his father to sow wheat in their land: and as his father sowed, the young child Jesus sowed also one corn of wheat. 2 And he reaped it and threshed it and made thereof an hundred measures (cors): and he called all the poor of the village unto the threshing-floor and gave them the wheat. And Joseph took the residue of the wheat. And he was eight years old when he wrought this sign.

XIII. 1 Now his father was a carpenter and made at that time ploughs and yokes. And there was required of him a bed by a certain rich man, that he should make it for him. And whereas one beam, that which installed the shifting one, was too short, and *Joseph* knew not what to do, the young child Jesus said to his father Joseph: Lay down the two pieces of wood and make them even at the next unto thee (*MSS.* at the middle part). And Joseph did as the young child said unto him. And Jesus stood at the other end and took hold upon the shorter beam and stretched and made it equal with the other. And his father Joseph saw it and marvelled: and he embraced the young child and kissed him, saying: Happy am I for that God hath given me this young child.

XIV. 1 But when Joseph saw the understanding of the child, and his age, that it was coming to the full, he thought with himself again that he should not be ignorant of letters; and he took him and delivered him to another teacher. And the teacher said unto Joseph: First will I teach him the Greek letters, and after that the Hebrew. For the teacher knew the skill of the child and was afraid of him: notwithstanding he wrote the alphabet and *Jesus* pondered thereon a long time [probably, "repeated it to him (Jesus) many times"] and answered him not. 2 And Jesus said to him: If thou be indeed a teacher, and if thou knowest letters well, tell me the power of the Alpha, and then I will tell thee the power of the Beta. And the teacher was provoked and smote him on the head. And the young child was hurt and cursed him, and straightway he fainted and fell to the ground on his face. 3 And the child returned unto the house of Joseph: and Joseph was grieved and commanded his mother, *saying:* Let him not forth without the door, for all they die that provoke him to wrath.

XV. 1 And after some time yet another teacher which was a faithful friend of Joseph said to him: Bring the young child unto me to the school; preadventure I may be able by cockering him to teach him the letters. And Joseph said: If thou hast no fear, my brother, take him with thee. And he took him with him, in fear and much trouble of spirit, but the young child followed him gladly. 2 And going with boldness into the school he found a book lying upon the pulpit and he took it, and read not the letters that were therein, but opened his mouth and spake by the Holy Spirit, and taught the law to them that stood by. And a great multitude came together and stood there hearkening, and marvelled at the beauty of his teaching and the readiness of his words, in that being an infant he uttered such things. 3 But when Joseph heard it, he was afraid, and ran unto the school, thinking whether this teacher also were without skill (*or* smitten with infirmity): but the teacher said unto Joseph: Know, my brother, that I received this child for a disciple, but he is full of grace and wisdom; and now I beseech thee, brother, take him unto thine house. 4 And when the young child heard that, he smiled upon him and said: Forasmuch as thou hast said well, and hast borne right witness, for thy sake shall he also that was smitten be healed. And forthwith the other teacher was healed. And Joseph took the young child and departed unto his house.

XVI. 1 And Joseph sent his son James to bind fuel and carry it into his house. And the young child Jesus also followed him. And as James was gathering of faggots, a viper bit the hand of James. 2 And as he was sore afflicted and ready to perish, Jesus came near and breathed upon the bite, and straightway the pain ceased, and the serpent burst, and forthwith James continued whole.

XVII. 1 And after these things, in the neighbourhood of Joseph, a little child fell sick and died, and his mother wept sore. And Jesus heard that there was great mourning and trouble, and he ran quickly and found the child dead: and he touched his breast and said: I say unto thee, Child, die not, but live and be with thy mother. And straightway it looked up and laughed. And he said to the woman: Take him up and give him milk, and remember me. 2 And the multitude that stood by saw it and marvelled, and said: of a truth this young child is either a god or an angel of God; for every word of his is a perfect work. And Jesus departed thence, and was playing with other children.

XVIII. 1 And after some time there was work of building. And there came a great tumult, and Jesus arose and went thither: and he saw a man lying dead, and took hold of his hand and said: Man, I say unto thee, arise and do thy work. And immediately he arose and worshipped him. 2 And when the multitude saw it, they were astonished, and said: this young child is from heaven: for he hath saved many souls from death, and hath power to save them all his life long.

XIX. 1 And when he was twelve years old his parents went according to the custom unto Jerusalem to the feast of the passover with their company: and after the passover they returned to go unto their house. And as they returned the child Jesus went back to Jerusalem; but his parents supposed that he was in their company. 2 And when they had gone a day's journey, they sought him among their kinsfolk, and when they found him not, they were troubled, and returned again to the city seeking him. And after the third day they found him in the temple sitting in the midst of the doctors and hearing and asking them *questions*. And all the men paid heed to him and marvelled how that being a young child he put to silence the elders and teachers of the people, expounding the heads of the law and the parables of the prophets. 3 And his mother Mary came near and said unto him: Child, wherefore hast thou so done unto us? behold we have sought thee sorrowing. And Jesus said unto them: why seek ye me? know ye not that I must be in my Father's house? 4 but the scribes and Pharisees said: Art thou the mother of this child? and she said: I am. And they said unto her: blessed art thou among women, because God hath blessed the fruit of thy womb. For such glory and such excellence and wisdom we have neither seen nor heard at any time.

5 And Jesus arose and followed his mother and was subject unto his parents: but his mother kept *in mind* all that came to pass. And Jesus increased in wisdom and stature and grace. Unto him be glory for ever and ever. Amen.

GREEK TEXT B

The Writing of the holy Apostle Thomas concerning the conversation of the Lord in his childhood.

I. I, Thomas, the Israelite, have thought it needful to make known unto all the brethren that are of the Gentiles the mighty works of childhood which our Lord Jesus Christ wrought when he was conversant in the body, and came unto the city of Nazareth in the fifth year of his age.

II. 1 On a certain day when there had fallen a shower of rain he went forth of the house where his mother was and played upon the ground where the waters were running: and he made pools, and the waters flowed down, and the pools were filled with water. Then saith he: I will that ye become clean and wholesome waters. And straightway they did so. 2 But a certain son of Annas the scribe passed by bearing a branch of willow, and he overthrew the pools with the branch, and the waters were poured out. And Jesus turned about and said unto him: O ungodly and disobedient one, what hurt have the pools done thee that thou hast emptied them? Thou shalt not finish thy course, and thou shalt be withered up even as the branch which thou hast in hand. 3 And he went on, and after a little he fell and gave up the ghost. And when the young children that played with him saw it, they marvelled and departed and told the father of him that was dead. And he ran and found the child dead, and went and accused Joseph.

III. 1 Now Jesus made of that clay twelve sparrows: and it was the sabbath day. And a child ran and told Joseph, saying: behold, thy child playeth about the brook, and hath made sparrows of the clay, which is not lawful. 2 And he when he heard it went and said to the child: Wherefore doest thou so and profaneth the sabbath? But Jesus answered him not, but looked upon the sparrows and said: Go ye, take your flight, and remember me in your life. And at the word they took flight and went up into the air. And when Jesus saw it he was astonished.

IV. 1 And after certain days, as Jesus passed through the midst of the city, a certain child cast a stone at him and smote his shoulder. And Jesus said unto him: thou shalt not finish thy course. And straightway he also fell down and died. And they that were there were amazed, saying: from whence is this child, that every word which he speaketh becometh a perfect work? 2 But they also departed and accused Joseph, saying: Thou wilt not be able to dwell with us in this city: but if thou wilt, teach thy child to bless and not to curse: for verily he slayeth our children: and everything that he saith becometh a perfect work.

V. And as Joseph sat upon his seat, the child stood before him; and he took hold upon his ear and pinched it sore. But Jesus looked upon him earnestly and said: It sufficeth thee.

VI. 1 And on the morrow he took him by the hand and led him to a certain teacher, Zacchaeus by name, and said unto him: Take this child, O master, and teach him letters. And the other said: Deliver him unto me, my brother, and I will teach him the scripture, and I will persuade him to bless all men and not to curse them. 2 And when Jesus heard that he laughed and said unto them: Ye speak that ye know, but I have knowledge more than you, for I am before the worlds. And I know when the fathers of your fathers were begotten, and I know how many are the years of your life. And *every* one that heard it was amazed. 3 And again saith Jesus unto them: Marvel ye because I said unto you that I know how many are the years of your life? Of a truth I know when the world was created. Behold, now ye believe me not: when ye shall see my cross, then will ye believe that I speak truth. And they were astonished when they heard all these things.

VII. 1 Now Zacchaeus wrote the alphabet in Hebrew, and saith unto him: Alpha. And the young child said: Alpha. And again the master said: Alpha, and the young child likewise. Then again the third time the master said: Alpha. Then Jesus looked upon the teacher and said: Thou that knowest not the Alpha, how can thou teach another the Beta? And the child beginning at the Alpha said of his own accord the two and twenty letters. 2 And thereafter saith he: Hear, O master, the ordinance of the first letter, and know how many incomings and lines it hath, and marks, common, going apart, and coming together. And when Zacchaeus heard such designations of the one letter he was amazed and had nothing to answer; and turning about he said unto Joseph: My brother, this child is of a truth not earthly born: take him away therefore from me.

VIII. 1 And after these things one day Jesus was playing with other boys upon the top of an house of two stories. And one child was pushed down by another and thrown to the ground and died. And the boys which were playing with him, when they saw it, fled, and Jesus was left alone standing upon the roof whence the boy was thrown down. 2 And when the parents of the boy that was dead heard of it they ran weeping, and when they found the boy lying dead upon the earth and Jesus standing alone, they supposed that the boy had been thrown down by him, and they looked upon him and reviled him. 3 But Jesus, seeing that, leaped down straightway from the upper story and stood at the head of him that was dead and saith to him: Zeno, did I cast thee down? Arise and tell. For so was the boy called. And with the word the boy rose up and worshipped Jesus and said: Lord, thou didst not cast me down, but when I was dead thou didst make me alive.

IX. 1 And a few days after one of the neighbours was cleaving wood and did cut off the sole of his foot with the axe, and by loss of blood was at the point to die. 2 And much people ran together and Jesus came thither with them. 3 And he took hold of the foot of the young man that was smitten, and healed him forthwith, and saith unto him: Arise, cleave thy wood. And he arose and worshiped him, giving thanks, and cleft the wood. Likewise also all those that were there marvelled and gave thanks unto him.

X. Now when he was six years old, Mary his mother sent him to fetch water from the spring: and as he went his pitcher was broken. And he went to the spring and spread out his upper garment and drew water out of the spring and filled it and took it and brought back the water to his mother. And she, when she saw it, was amazed and embraced him and kissed him.

XI. 1 And when he came to the eighth year of his age Joseph was required by a certain rich man to build him a bed, for he was a carpenter. And he went forth into the field to gather wood, and Jesus also went with him. And he cut two beams of wood and wrought them with the axe, and set one beside the other and measured and found it too short; and when he saw that he was vexed and sought to find another. 2 But Jesus seeing it saith unto him: Set these two together so that the ends of both be even. And Joseph, though he was perplexed concerning this, what the child should mean, did that which was commanded. And he saith again unto him: Take firm hold of the short beam. And Joseph took hold on it, marvelling. Then Jesus also took hold of the other end and pulled the [other] end thereof and made it also equal to the other beam, and saith unto Joseph: Be no more vexed, but do thy work without hindrance. And he when he saw it was exceedingly amazed, and said within himself: Blessed am I for that God hath given me such a son. 3 And when they departed into the city Joseph told it to Mary, and she when she heard and saw the wonderful mighty works of her son, rejoiced, glorifying him.

With the Father and the Holy Spirit now and for ever and world without end. Amen.

Five

CONCLUSION

The material contained in this volume by no means exhausts the literature that might be used to illustrate the development of the Jesus legend. It is sufficient to show, however, that the *historical* Jesus did not long endure in the memory either of members or enemies of the cult of Christ. The needs of the early church—defensive strategies as well as missionary outreach—combined to ensure that the historical Jesus would remain shrouded and irrecoverably buried. Only the hopes of his followers escaped the tomb. Already by Paul's day, the real reasons for the execution of Jesus had been displaced by the belief that his death could not be explained in merely human terms—only in terms of a secret purpose "ordained by God from the beginning of the world." It is the irony underlying the composition of the Gospels—indeed their *raison d'être*—that it was Jesus' death, and not his life, that saved him from obscurity.

Schweitzer once cautioned that the historical Jesus—were he ever to be discovered—would be very different from the Christ of the church's invention.[1] He would not be the God-man of the church fathers, the gentle Jesus of Sunday-school piety, the fierce pantocrator of Eastern iconography, nor even the political rebel glorified in the German Friedensbewegung. But as Schweitzer's miscalculations have shown, it is far easier to say what the historical Jesus was not than what he was, to disallow what is historically improbable than to construct an image free of improbabilities.

Some scholars would consider it extravagant even to conclude that Jesus lived and died in Judea during the Roman occupation—although Christian and non-Christian sources commonly agree on this point. Beyond this, almost no aspect of Jesus' life is indisputable. We cannot be certain whether he was "crucified *under* Pontius Pilate,"[2] as the Gospels grudgingly acknowledge, or was stoned as a heretic by his fellow Jews, as the Talmud wants to suggest. We have lost sight of the major charge against him—even though a threat against the Temple seems plausible.

As to the substance of his teaching, we are scarcely better informed, though it appears he preached the coming of the Kingdom, dabbled in making predictions about the time of its arrival, and ran afoul of the rabbis. Though he did not found a church or provide instructions for a community of believers, he may have initiated an apocalyptic preaching movement in Galilee.

Even the "radical" view that Jesus began as a disciple of John is not immune from criticism, since Josephus knows nothing of the connection, and the Gospels use John's "testimony" as a way of securing Jesus' prestige. Thus, that there was any connection between the two figures can be doubed.

Going further back, we come to the birth legends, late and contradictory and wholly lacking in historical value. Here too, we must search for Jesus in the crack between what the Jews were saying about the circumstances of his birth and the Christian response to the slander, in the Gospels. What emerges is the name Jesus itself, the name of his mother, Miriam, and an early tradition—which the Gospels strain to overcome—of his illegitimacy. I would add to this one additional piece of information only because there seems no good reason to doubt it, namely that Jesus came from Galilee. Given the bad reputation of the region in the early first century as the "region of unbelievers" (*Gala' ha goyim*), it is hard to imagine why such a provenance would have been invented.

The picture of Jesus that has emerged in the twentieth century, lacking in detail though it may be, is that of an itinerant first-century preacher who announced the end of the world and the judgment of God on the faithless and wicked of his generation. To ascertain this much and no more is a discomfort to those who look to history for the vindication of their beliefs and hopes, a discomfort not different in kind from that experienced by the Jesus-believers when faced with the humiliation and death of their master. Such discomforts lead today, as they led in the distant past, to a retreat from history and from reason, and to certainties that are only possible as a consequence of neglect. Christianity arose as a religion of solace and comfort, a myth designed to dry the tears of the afflicted, the superstitious, and the disinherited.

The endurance of this myth long after its credibility has been exploded does not point to the literature of the New Testament as truth of a higher order, but to the unchanging conditions of humanity that make the religious myth necessary.

NOTES

Two: The Delay in Writing the Gospels

1. See Geza Vermes, *The Dead Sea Scrolls in English* (Baltimore: Penguin, 1962).

2. Ps. 22; Jer. 18:1-3; Zech. 11:12-13 (Judas' betrayal); Deut. 21:6-9; and notably Isa. 53.

3. See "Q," pericope 59, p. 96.

4. Josephus, *Antiquities of the Jews* 18.5.2.

5. See 2 Kings 1:8; Zech. 13:4; Isa. 40:3; and Mal. 3:1; 4:5.

6. Acts 18:25; see also Luke 7:18-23, a passage which indicates that John's followers remained unconvinced that Jesus was the Messiah. A remnant of this sect survives in modern Iraq, the Mandaeans.

7. The culpable offense is best preserved in Luke 23:5: "He stirs up the people, teaching throughout Judea, from Galilee even to this place." The charge therefore was insurrection (see also Mark 15:7).

8. I refer to the anachronistic interpretations of the fundamentalist sects. Confronted with the verse "This generation will live to see it all . . ." such sects deny the empirical falsity of the prediction by projecting the event into the near future.

9. I regard only five of the letters ascribed to Paul as coming more or less directly from him: 1 Thessalonians; Romans; 1 and 2 Corinthians, and Galatians.

10. See the *Acts of Pilate* in M. R. Jones, *The Apochryphal New Testament* (Oxford: Oxford University Press, 1924), pp. 117-140.

11. Josephus, *Antiquities of the Jews*, 18.3.1.

12. We need only point to the "meaning" of the number 666, as-

signed to the "beast" in Rev. 13:17-18: the numerical tally of the letters in Nero's name (spelled in Hebrew) and a reference to the practice of requiring homage to the emperor as a qualification for citizenship.

13. For the early church, the practice of "prophet killing" was thought to extend from Abel down to Zechariah (see Acts 4:25).

14. A further volume in this series will explore the Gospel tradition in depth and a final collection of the responses to the Jesus myth by pagan philosophers and writers.

15. A good summary of the sociology of the early Christian movement is provided by Wayne Meeks, *The First Urban Christians* (New Haven: Yale University Press, 1983).

16. Origen, *Contra Celsum*, trans. Henry Chadwick (Cambridge: Cambridge University Press, 1953), 1.9; 3.44.

Three: Jesus Outside the Gospels

1. Reimarus, *Fragments*, ed. C. H. Talbert (Philadelphia: Fortress, 1970), pp. 72-73.

2. The two main forms of the Talmud, Babylonian and Palestinian, are similar but not identical in content; by most reckonings, the Palestinian Talmud was formed earlier than the Babylonian, work continuing on the latter well after the fifth century of the Christian era.

3. For an explanation of the abbreviations adopted here, see R. T. Herford, *Christianity in Talmud and Midrash* (New York: KTAV, 1903), p. xv.

4. Ibid., p. 37.

5. See Herford's long discussion of this passage, pp. 58-61.

6. The account given here is abbreviated from Joseph Klausner, *Jesus of Nazareth* (London: 1925), pp. 48-51.

7. Klausner, *Jesus of Nazareth*, pp. 51-53.

8. James M. Robinson, ed., *The Nag Hammadi Library in English* (Leiden: Brill, 1977).

9. Ibid.

10. Those interested in pursuing the conclusions of the Dutch School should consult Pierre van Paasen, *Why Jesus Died* (New York, 1959).

11. The most thorough discussion of the subject is to be found in B. H. Streeter, *The Four Gospels, a Study of Origins* (Oxford: Oxford University

Press, 1924).

12. See A. M. Farrer, "On Dispensing with Q" in *Studies in the Gospels* (Oxford: Oxford University Press, 1955), pp. 55-86.

Four: The Growth of the Jesus Myth

1. Though the "historical" Jesus was probably a thaumaturge or wonder-worker. On the evidence for this, see the excellent study by Morton Smith, *Jesus the Magician* (New York: 1978).

2. Most if not all of the New Testament miracles have close parallels in Classical and Near Eastern literature and belong to the common stock of ancient folklore. See D. L. Dungan, *Documents for the Study of the Gospels* (Philadelphia: Fortress, 1980).

Five: Conclusion

1. Albert Schweitzer, *The Quest of the Historical Jesus* (New York: Macmillan, 1968), p. 399.

2. The phrase *sub Pontio Pilato* in the creed is no more than a historical marker: the phrase "by Pontius Pilate" was studiously avoided.